The Five

an Answer to
the Christian Identity Crisis

By Vince Corcoran

The Five: an Answer to the Christian Identity Crisis
by Vince Corcoran

Cover Design: Vince Corcoran
Cover Photography: Jorik Blom

ISBN – 978-1497375031

For more information email:
encounterculturemninistries@gmail.com

TABLE OF CONTENTS

Dedication

This book is dedicated to the students of MorningStar University – past, present and future. Before I was one of you, you inspired me. When I was one of you, you changed me. When I was your instructor, you taught me. May you become greater than you imagine is possible and be part of fulfilling Revelation 11:15.

Thanks

For my life, my vibrant upbringing, and my confidence, I thank my parents – Jim and Charmane.

For their spiritual imprint on my life, I thank Eddie Reynolds, Mike Thompson, Nathaniel Smith, Steve Thompson, Rick Joyner, Stephen Alls, Jason Hooper, Nathan Scott, Briskilla Zananiri, Elizabeth Braswell, and Brad McClendon.

For their contributions to this book, I thank Sarah Godwin, Allison Davenport, Joe Shrewsbury, my parents, Michael Coller, and all my interns.

For enduring me in my victories and enjoying me in my bruising battles, I thank Kidd and Niki Corcoran, Jeremy and Ashley Shuck, Nate and Natalie Shaver, Michael Miller, Craig Fuhrmann, Yuri Nosenko, Kinzel Cassady, Cole Mackie, Andrew Armstrong, Jordan Hill, and Scott McClelland.

And for stalking me with His lovingkindness and for letting me trip on the waves, I thank Jesus.

Endorsements

"This book is crucial for this time in the Church. We are about to see the Five-Fold Ministry renewed in the Church, and Vince carefully explains how each of us can step into our five-fold role. It is rare to find such a practical "how-to" manual for developing and practicing the five-fold ministry that is easily understood by believers of all backgrounds and experience. It is time for us to find our proper place in the Body of Christ, and this book is a great first step toward that end."

Joe Shrewsbury
MorningStar Prophetic Ministries Leader
Fort Mill, SC

"The revelation of the Five as personality types helped me understand myself and my ministry calling much more clearly. Our God is truly creative and intentional in how He forms each one of us. Vince Corcoran masterfully illuminates the different types of people God has designed and how they can work together as an effective team. I highly recommend this book for anyone who feels called to leadership in any area of life."

Michael Coller
Unveiled Church Senior Pastor
Grand Rapids, MI

Foreword

Enlist. Equip. Empower. Engage™.

I remember the moment the Lord spoke these four words to me like it was yesterday. We were in the middle of a conference and it came from out of nowhere into my spirit. I wrote them down and proceeded to doodle them in journals for months and months to come. One day, I wrote down e4 and drew a circle around it and realized that it was an Ephesians 4 mandate...call me slow. As I grabbed my Bible and discovered that all of these words were explicitly defined in this Scripture I knew that part of my life mission had just been revealed.

To pick up Vince's book and see this Ephesians 4 mandate woven throughout thrilled me to no end. Like never before, the body of Christ MUST know WHO we are, WHO is in us, and what our part is in this great race. We are in desperate need of an awareness and an awakening to our identity in Christ.

Ephesians 4 starts out with Paul beseeching us to walk worthy of the calling in which we were called. He is not asking politely or merely making a suggestion. That word "beseech" means to beg, to implore, to exhort, to summon. It is time for us to answer the call to this exhortation and to arise, walking together, honoring one another, loving one another, and knowing that unity is the key that will keep us at peace.

As someone who was and is a part of this young man's life, I am so proud of him for completing this first book of many. His heart to pour into others and see them released into the fullness of truth permeates throughout. I have loved to watch Vince go after the Lord in such a way that he, like Paul, can call himself a prisoner of the Lord and one who, with all that is in him, desires to walk worthy of the calling.

This book will help so many people understand who they are and how they were made and WHY they are like they are. I can see small groups sitting around talking about The Five...pondering the differences and how beautifully they all work together. May you be blessed beyond measure as you read these words and may you get a glimpse of yourself and the way the Father made you so that you, too, can walk worthy, get engaged in culture around you and release change everywhere you go.

Elizabeth Braswell
Founder, ebraswell & company

My Natural Tribe: Exploring the Need for Identity

The Power of a Superhuman Identity

The story of Christianity is a story of two human races. When Adam was created, he carried within him the entirety of humanity. When Adam ate the fruit of the knowledge of good and evil, the first Adamic race fell into a natural state of self-focused fear. The Last Adam, Jesus, walked into a locked room of men who were gripped by fear. He breathed on them and inaugurated the Last race of humanity. Weeks later their new nature would more fully manifest at the day of Pentecost, but the First Born of Many Brethren had given them all they needed to re-institute the original purposes of man – be fruitful, multiply and take over the world.

Peter, John and Paul wrote to many different groups and individuals about living as members of this new race of men. The letters that they and others wrote make up the majority of the New Testament. To the Corinthian Christians, Paul wrote a rebuke that they were acting as "mere men" in their treatment of each other (1 Corinthians 3:3). In a later letter, he encouraged them saying that "if any man is in Christ, he is a new creature" (2 Corinthians 5:17). John the beloved wrote in his later years, that we have confidence in the context of God's perfect love before the Lord on the day of judgment, because "as He is, so are we in this world" (1 John 4:17).

It is evident, throughout the entire New Testament, that we are not just humans; we are supernatural humans, with supernatural gifts, because we possess the exact same Spirit as Jesus (1 Corinthians 6:17). We are drawn to superhero movies because they are pale reflections of who we are. What makes us different from the superheroes of the world's media is that the nature of our supernatural abilities is love and self-control, not control of others. While the superhuman powers of our imaginations are things like influencing someone's thoughts or controlling objects or people without touching them, Jesus walked through walls, walked on water and gave free life to those He touched. And Jesus said that those who believe would do even greater things than He did (John 14:12).

Towards the end of Paul's ministry, in one of his more personal letters to a young leader of one of his churches, Paul told Timothy to be like a good soldier by not entangling himself in "civilian affairs" (2 Timothy 2:4). Likewise, in order to live as supernatural people, we must be careful to be caught up in the ways of the King and His Kingdom. This will inevitably cause us to be increasingly unimpressed with and unaffected by the things that do not matter. It would be a strange thing for a soldier to call home while at war and ask about the neighborhood gossip. Paul also uses the analogy of an athlete. The focus and attention of a professional athlete is solely on the goal at hand, not the uniform of their opponents, the ticket sales of the event or the reaction of the crowd. If their attention does drift to such things, they become ineffective. The same applies to us.

This is not tunnel vision, but rather it is intentionality, diligence, and faithfulness to the cause that we carry. It is the ultimatum of a King coming to reclaim a planet. This cause is our motivation; it is our lifeline. When we are part of something far bigger than ourselves, we catch a vision for greatness and partnership. We forget about our selves, we forget about our ambitions, and we look to our ultimate goal. Our perspective changes and we find ourselves having wider vision after all, because we have removed the things that distract us. With this wider vision and greater perspective comes greater clarity – about everything and everyone around us.

Our values changes when we attach ourselves to something greater. Like a new parent who had great plans for a hobby or even a career, when that beautiful child arrives, those plans evaporate. The parent's time, energy, and resources flood away from anything but their baby. The presence of something transcendent will always eclipse the faded importance of the transient.

As we set aside things that we have valued for so long, sacrificing the things we loved for the One we love, we agree with Paul in saying that everything we once held dear we now count as worthless in comparison to what is coming. Intentional focus on the awesome future makes even our greatest accomplishments seem as impressive as stacking cow-pies and banana peels.

Even beyond increased motivation and focus, being connected to something as epic as global conquest inspires personal confidence in one's identity. It is one thing to love a sports team. It is a whole other thing to work for a sports franchise, let alone be on the team itself. But we are not second-string benchwarmers; we are the stars, the starting line-up. With what the writer of Hebrews calls "a great cloud of witnesses," all eyes are on us and all of creation is groaning in anticipation of us walking out our identities as children of God (Hebrews 12:1 and Romans 8:19). We are not merely children of our ancestors; we are direct descendants of God Himself because we were born a second time when we received the Holy Spirit as a promise of an inheritance in Christ.

Access to such a great inheritance and the riches of an unshakable Kingdom make the things of this present, perverted age look so unappealing. Who would want a rusty bicycle with a flat tire when they are offered their choice of any brand new sports car? It changes our value systems, our expectations and our focus when we know who we are in Him. Not only are we superheroes, we are the Bride of Christ, the sons of God and the very Body of Christ. If any group of people should be confident, it ought to be us.

It happened with the first generation of Saints. In the book of Acts, Jesus' disciples were put on trial for their exploits of salvation and healing. They confidently confronted the religious leaders, saying that they could do nothing but continue to preach a Jesus revolution. It says that the leaders observed their confidence and "knew that they had been with Jesus" (Acts 4:13). This is what many of us have lacked – true encounter with Jesus that unwraps boldness, confidence and courage. We can study concepts and debate theology until we are blue-faced, but when someone smarter or more persuasive than us comes along, our knowledge will fail. However, when we are told who we are by Jesus and when we are identified and commissioned by the Author of history, nothing will sway us from our course.

Even Jesus Needed a Name Tag: Adamic Brothers as Examples

Our identity is so essential to our destiny, that without knowing and understanding ourselves as revealed by God, we will wander into error and sin every time. It doesn't matter what our context is, in order to take ground in any arena – in society or within ourselves – our foundational beliefs about ourselves will set the stage for what transpires. This issue of identity is what distinguishes Adam's sons from Jesus' brothers.

In the garden, God gave Adam a wonderful life. He had places to explore, to cultivate, and to develop. Adam was not lacking tasks or purpose. What he did lack was a companion, someone to relate to, and join with. He knew what he was supposed to do. When the man had his wife, he knew who she was, and they had purpose. One of the primary tactics that the serpent used then, and continues to use now on us, is to attack the character and identity of God.

Adam didn't need to think about himself; God was the One who saw the problem – Adam needed Eve. They were designed to be like God, but the moment they began to doubt, evaluate, and question God's identity, that was the moment they became self-focused. This self-focus was a result of insecurity in the identity of the One from whom they were hewn. Once His identity was called into question their identity was open to be challenged as well. This brought them into agreement with the father of lies.

Fast-forward several thousand years; the Last Adam is born to a young Middle Eastern girl. She knew who He was, but she stored that up in her own heart. At Jesus' baptism, when He was about to step into the fullest expression of His identity the Father did not speak from Heaven and tell Him what He would *do*.

Rather, His Father told Him who He *is*. He bestowed identity on Him. In both Mark and Luke's gospels, the Father addresses Jesus directly saying, "You are my beloved Son. In You I am well-pleased." He wasn't saying this for the benefit of the people, nor did He even tell Him what to do. Jesus would then follow His Father around for the next three years, doing only what He saw His Father doing (John 5:19).

In that moment, Jesus and the Father and the Holy Spirit joined together to reset what had been lost with Adam. They started a new race, one that would redeem and save the first race of men. They laid the foundation for this race with an emphasis on who we are and how He feels about us. This is not to imply that God made a mistake – that is not the point. The point is that at the very center of humanity is a need to be told who we are and how God feels about us. Adam had perfect conditions and forgot his identity. Jesus had horrible conditions and was told His identity. Both changed the world. Both were the firstborn of a race of men. But One saved the other. And it was the One who was told His identity who was and will be successful.

Tribes:
Purpose and Position from History and Heritage

One of the hardest things for Gentile believers is appreciating the Old Testament. We know that it is important, especially when we read something in the New Testament that is confusing, but it is essential to our understanding of God to know how He has related to the first human race since the beginning and thereby set us up for redemption through the last superhuman race. Not only does the Old Testament set the stage for the New Testament, but it also provides true stories of real people to illustrate the revelations of the New Covenant and attempts to show what God is like. The Old Testament Scriptures are full of prophetic signs and symbols that point to Jesus. The patterns and situations in the Scriptures are shadows of what is to come (Hebrews 10:1).

The Twelve Tribes of Israel were physical, but their names and natures had spiritual implications. At the end of his life, Israel prophesied over each of his sons. The words that he spoke over each would carry authoritative weight, not only for the rest of their lives, but even to this day in the lives of their descendants for generations to follow. We see it especially in the word he spoke over Judah. In each phrase that Israel used in his word over his son Judah, we see a detail of the life and ministry of Jesus' first and second coming. Reading through each of the sons' prophetic word we find references to what Jesus did, was, will do or ever will be.

As with any organization, the leaders of each tribe would set the course and personality of their tribe. These prophetic declarations of Israel carried into the corporate psyche of each tribe. Whether these kinds of pronouncements are predictive or creative in nature is the age-old debate about the prophetic ministry, but we can see them in small instances, like in the case of Levi. Israel said that his son Levi was a violent man (Genesis 49:5). This was because of Levi's history; he and his brother Simeon had killed a group of Hivites because of an offense they had towards a prince named Shechem – who had eyes for their sister (Genesis 34). That violence would come in handy when, in the desert, Israel was in rebellion and the Levites were the ones who stood with Moses and the Lord. The Levites unreservedly killed their fellow Israelites who had turned from the Lord. The Lord gave the priesthood to those Levites (Exodus 32).

Not only do the physical tribe divisions have spiritual implications, directing the attitudes, tendencies and personalities of Israel's tribes, but it also happens with our denominations today. Those who have started movements that became denominations had certain things that the Lord put on their hearts as "the most important thing," and they lived out that message so radically that others followed them by taking on the same value systems. The Baptist churches are called "Baptists" because in their history, their leaders have valued baptism above everything else. "Bible" churches, likewise, value Biblical teaching. "Charismatics" value the charismatic gifts of the Spirit. As much as we may not like the division that can come from denominations, if one group doesn't do their part to hold the line on their values, those values will be lost. We need each other.

Additionally, the spiritual tribe that we find ourselves in has great physical implications as well. Where you are ordained to live and what you are anointed to do are inseparably interconnected. I have a friend who has been connected to some very charismatic churches and movements, but the Lord has planted him at the epicenter of a very traditional church region. Part of his calling is to be an influence on the traditional evangelical church. I have another friend who loves, no, adores theology, but he is planted in a large charismatic church. He is a light to those around him, showing people that "theology" and "doctrine" are not Christian cuss words, but that studying the things of God is meant to unlock our hearts. When he teaches, and when I have had long theological discussions with him, I find my heart falling more in love with Jesus, not more cold and dogmatic.

In both of these cases, my friends have been assigned by the Lord to affect the culture around them with what they carry as a value. And in both cases, the culture around them is not inclined towards their values. If we are connected to the heartbeat of God, we will be drawn in one way or another to places that need what we carry as a value. We carry these values because of the purposes we have received from God. He prepares us to walk out these purposes by training us in places and situations that cultivate in us the values necessary to transform the situations we are placed in. Once we have sufficiently gotten what we needed from our initial training, God will transition us to a testing ground where we will be put into positions that require us to draw from the training He gave us through our families and experiences.

Human Tendency vs. Superhuman Tendency: Segregation or Unification

By nature, we have a tendency to be carnal, selfish, and temporal in our thinking. When Adam ate the fruit in the garden, the first thing man did was look at themselves, evaluate their situations according to a self-preservation mentality, and hide themselves from perceived harm. We have not stopped evaluating and protecting ourselves since then, except in rare occasions of inspiration from the divine nature hidden deep inside us as image-bearers.

Living carnally, or in the flesh, is self-focus and self-centeredness. Before Adam fell, they were like God. God does not obsessively think of Himself. He is not self-focused. In fact, Jesus' death on the Cross was a statement saying, "Your lives are each more important than Mine. I will die so that you can live." When we live "according to the flesh," we agree with that statement in an unhealthy way. We satisfy our desires because we are valuing our will above His will.

This selfishness is a disease that keeps us stuck in the immediate present, with no vision for the future. And if somehow we start to think of the future, we are still striving to have a pleasant "now" – a "now" that has not yet happened. We become temporally minded, which has more to do with what realm of existence we are focused on than it has to do with time. Eternity is a realm, a world beyond our world. We think of Eternity in terms of time, because in our future "Eternity" will eventually be fully joined with earth. So to live temporally is to live as though that is never going to happen, or at least not in our lifetimes. This has been the attack of our enemy on those who study and focus on the End Times. The accusation is that Eschatology is irrelevant even though it is probably the most relevant subject we can put our time to studying. Relevant not because of what is coming, but because of Who is coming. There is a special crown of righteousness that will be given to those who "love His appearing" (2 Timothy 4:8).

As we submit to the Spirit, becoming more and more transformed into Christ's likeness, which we are predestined to become (Romans 8:29), we will become increasingly superhuman in every facet of our lives. Paul wrote to the Saints in Rome, explaining that the ways of the flesh and the ways of the Spirit are diametrically opposed to each other (Romans 8:6). James wrote that friendship or agreement with the ways of the world is "hatred towards God" (James 4:4). When we were still in our sin, entangled in the nature of the world and ruled by our flesh, we agree with its hatred toward God. However, we are not supposed to start hating the world that He made and paid to save, and call that "loving God." We are now in Christ, we are a new creation. We are in love with God, and we actually begin to love the world, too – just like He loved the world so much that He sent Jesus (John 3:16).

The tendency of super-humans is not to disconnect from the world and become spiritual, but to become so in touch with the eternal realm that we cannot separate this world from Eternity in our minds. Super-humans are not less physical and more spiritual; super-humans are more spiritually minded and therefore more in tune with the physical realm around them. Not surprisingly, Jesus was the perfect example of this. He was so spiritually minded that He was constantly aware of what was going on around Him. When a woman touched His cloak in a large crowd, and spiritual life came out of Him, He felt it leave Him physically when she was healed (Luke 8:46). Similarly, knowing in His Spirit that Lazarus was supposed to die so that He could resurrect Lazarus, He responded to a cry to hurry by waiting (John 11). Throughout the gospels we see time after time that He responded in the physical realm to what He saw the Father doing in the Eternal realm.

Superhuman perspective is a holistic perspective, but it is also a powerfully selfless perspective. Paul writes to one city and tells them to drop their lawsuits with each other with the simple logic "why not just be wronged?" (1 Corinthians 6:7) Then to another city he writes, "consider others more important than yourself" (Philippians 2:3). Clearly, our self-centered Western culture has missed something. Jesus taught, "Blessed are the peacemakers, for they shall be called sons of God" (Matthew 5:9). In other words, we will display our identity as members of the Divine Family with access and authority when we create peace in the midst of murderous and chaotic situations. Our nature – the way that we respond to situations – changes when we become more and more connected to the Father of the Divine Family. We begin to think less about ourselves and more about those around us, just like the Firstborn showed His love by living with our good as His goal.

However selfless a human can act, apart from the Divine Nature within, people will always operate out of fear. One manifestation of this fear is the human tendency toward segregation. Whether by race, socio-economic status, or belief system, we live as 'mere men' when we huddle with people that are just like us and judge everyone else for their differences. This is based in self-preservation and elitism that is a masquerade to hide insecurity. Those around us give us a false sense of safety, because we can use them as an emotional or social human shield to validate our beliefs or actions when those beliefs or actions get challenged.

In the Divine Family, there is this beautiful thing called "unity." We are the "body of Christ," which only works fully when all of the members are connected rightly and understand their individual functions and positions. Human nature is to break up into similar pieces, but superhuman nature is to be rightly connected to the correct parts in the correct ways. In the analogy of the anatomy, if a body acted out of human tendency, we would have a pile of bones, a pile of muscles, a pile of veins and a pile of organs. And the big, important bones would be on one side of the pile, not touching the dinky, little joint bones. The major organs wouldn't be caught dead associating with the lesser, unnecessary organs like the appendix or the tonsils.

Now, obviously, a body in segregation like this would not be a body at all. But that is how we have tried to function for a large chunk of Church history. We have been segregated into denominations, operating out of fear that we won't get the honor we are due or that we would lose congregants because they may find that they fit better somewhere else. But the Lord is restoring unity in the body of Christ. We are learning how to relate to each other by celebrating and preferring one another according to our strengths, and not judging each other according to our shortcomings. Differences in beliefs are not a reason to divide, but rather as a reason to unite. If each denomination upholds their part of the Church's calling, we will take over the world, people will know us by our love, and the kingdoms of this world will become the kingdoms of our God and His Christ. Then Jesus will return to the earth, we will take 1,000 years to prepare for the Father to live on earth with us, and we will unite Eternity fully with earth. But first we must love, appreciate and celebrate each other. That starts with understanding ourselves and discerning the other parts of the Body.

Man-Worship: Historically Unhealthy Relating to "the Fivefold"

One of the most insidious sins is pride. It was the downfall of Lucifer, and he has used it against us ever since that first time we came into agreement with Him. If our enemy cannot get us to stop driving down the path of life, then he will get us to drive recklessly down the highway of holiness and miss important stops along the way. For those who are highly motivated and successful in ministry, business and other respected realms of life, the attack has been to think highly of these people and honor them above others. For centuries now, we have struggled with elitism. Those that operate in the more visible areas of our churches get more honor than those that do the hard work behind the scenes. Paul said that more honor is due to the members of the body that are less public. He even said that those who do double work, teaching in the church and preaching outside the church, are due a double honorarium for their diligent service (1 Timothy 5:17).

This concept of rewarding those who are on the "front lines" and those who are "behind the scenes" is not just part of the New Covenant. In King David's day, those who went out to the battle got an equal portion of reward as those who stayed in the camp (1 Samuel 30:24). They were one army and the compensation was not based on performance or position or even on willingness; those who stayed with the baggage were too tired to go and fight (1 Samuel 30:21). The man who rushed into the battle first or killed the most men got rewarded, as did the man who stayed in the camp, checking to make sure the tents didn't blow away or that food was ready for the fighters when they returned. This is an attitude that we need to readopt in the 21st Century Church.

Looking at Ephesians 4, where we have been introduced to the "Fivefold Ministry Offices," in order to understand how to rightly relate to the Five it is important to see what their stated purpose is. "And He gave some as apostles, and some as prophets, and some as evangelists, and some as pastors and teachers, for the equipping of the saints for the works of service, to the building up of the body of Christ; until we all attain to the unity of the faith, and the knowledge of the Son of God, to the mature man, to the measure of the stature which belongs to the fullness of Christ."

The Five were given to the Body of Christ for everyone's benefit. Their purpose is to equip those around them to do what they do, to strengthen everyone around them until everyone is unified, knows Jesus really well, is walking in maturity, and full of the virtuous character and attitude of Jesus Christ.

Historically, we have looked at these Five as super-Christians. And if we are not careful, we will feed the elitism that plagues the world. God gives authority so that leaders can serve those over whom they have authority. Jesus, the Man with the most authority ever, came to serve (Matthew 20:28). And to His friends, He said that if they wanted to grow in authority, they would become the servant of everyone around them (Mark 9:35). The Five are personality Tribes, but if we view the Five as ministries, we must realize that they are ministries of service, not ministries of responsibility or even leadership. Paul told Timothy to "do the *work* of an evangelist" (2 Timothy 4:5), because it is hard work. Ministry is not all fun and games and glory. There are parts of occupational ministry positions that are very taxing and require endurance.

If we are to grow from generation to generation, we must elevate people into our places that can and will surpass us. A father whose son does not live a happier, more secure life has failed to raise him well. It must be the goal of each generation to accelerate its successor beyond itself, for if it doesn't the success of the first generation is lost and the foundation it laid will have to be rebuilt.

Jesus knew this and told those that He was raising up that they were going to do greater works than the ones that He did (John 14:12). It is an insult to be given the knowledge, wisdom and understanding that someone gained through experience and not use that impartation as a launching pad into greater and higher things. Consider this in terms of technology, if our children said that they would not use the Internet or the vast array of technological advances that we created simply because they wanted to do it themselves, that would be a detrimental loss. The ceiling of our fathers' generation is our floor, just as our ceiling will be the floor for our children. It is an honor for a father to have a son that becomes more successful than he had become.

We are therefore very thankful for the revelations, the studies and the teachings of our ancestors in the faith. Without them, we would not have what we have now. What you will read in the following chapters is not a correction of what has been said, but an addition. Where we have had an unhealthy attitude towards "Apostles," "Prophets," "Evangelists," "Pastors," and "Teachers" as super-Christian ministers, my hope is that you will begin to see the greatness of the Five in yourself. Where we have unintentionally worshipped the "man of God," my prayer is that we would turn and worship the "God of man."

The next five chapters will take each of the Five and explore them in detail. We will look at them academically, as each of the titles are used in Scripture and attempt to define them in our context. We will look at how they each think, how they each act, their unique strengths and weaknesses, as well as some examples – Biblical, historical and fictional. Think of them as Five Tribes, groupings of people that have similar ways of relating to the world around them. They are ultimately the same race of people, but have a certain bent based on how they grew up and were designed.

After we put the microscope on each of the Five, we will take a step back and look at how the Five work in the microcosm of churches. Then we will take another step back to see how the Five function in non-church settings. This will help us to put the puzzle pieces together by looking at how to relate to others in the context of the Five as personality Tribes. We will wrap it all together in the last chapters by holding up a mirror to see which of the Five fits you best and then celebrate the freedom we have to be unique and praiseworthy just as we are.

Avoiding "churchy" language is a difficult task when attempting to define, or re-define, concepts and terminology that have been used for centuries. This is not an academic book; it is an identity book. The most important outcome is that you would find freedom in understanding and loving the person that God created you to be. Secondarily, if you come to understand and love the people around you more, then this book will have been a major success. May the Holy Spirit guide and help you to these ends.

The Parable of Ecclon

Jesus is the ultimate example for us in all things. His primary method for teaching in the gospels was telling a story to the masses and then explaining it to His disciples. If it worked for Him, I suspect it is a good idea to follow His lead. The following story is a dense parable that we will come back to at the beginning of each of the next five chapters to explain the Five. Enjoy the story as it develops throughout this book.

The people of Ecclon were the happiest people on earth. It's true, no one ever went hungry, everyone did meaningful work, but also had more fun than anyone in the valley could imagine. The Ecclonian children were smart, mature, free, and humble. Their parents lived long, looked young, and smiled without trying. The only problem that they had was that they didn't have enough area on the mountainside to accommodate all the visitors that they adopted into their community. They had outgrown their village – a happiness epidemic.

The chief leader of Ecclon, Joshua, called a meeting to discuss a solution. After careful deliberation, they decided that the valley towns of Fort Follis and Benton could use a neighboring town between them. The town would be named New Ecclon and would rest at the base of the opposite mountain – south of Fort Follis and north of the river town Benton.

It would take a team of people to create New Ecclon. Joshua appointed his twin brother, Andrew, to lead a group of Ecclonians to colonize the valley. Andrew chose this team carefully. His decisions on team members were based primarily on friendship, but Joshua heartily agreed with each choice as the best options available. When Andrew saw Joshua's list, the lists were identical. This was a great sign for the success of New Ecclon.

Of those selected to colonize the valley, the most difficult for Joshua to let go of was his sister, Piper. She would serve as a communicator between the two villages, splitting her time 50-50 with each of her brothers. She was the youngest and the only daughter in the family – Ecclon's princess. Confident in her family's love and strongly opinionated, Piper always spoke her mind and seemed to see things from a unique perspective. She had an uncanny knack for seeing a problem before it became a problem. Piper was an "old soul" with unique and refreshing perspective and insight. Her brothers adored her and trusted her implicitly.

The most exciting recruit was a couple, Evan and Angela. They had met in Ecclon while each were passing through. They instantly fell in love with each other and their new mountain home. If ever there were a couple that enjoyed life to the fullest degree, it was Evan and Angela. They were constantly hiking the mountain trails and bringing back friends. At their wedding, Joshua said, "I blame the overwhelming growth of Ecclon mostly on Evan and Angela's hiking addiction," with a smirk and a wink. Andrew knew that for New Ecclon to succeed, they would be a vital part of keeping things new and fresh.

The one leader that Ecclon's residents would miss the most would be Patrick. Patrick was a loving man with a propensity to adopt anything with a pulse; he would bring his family of seven and many animals. Patrick and his wife were young for having five children, but they made everyone feel like part of their family. Patrick and Andrew were neighbors in Ecclon, and despite the age gap between them, Andrew knew that no one exemplified the heart of Ecclon like Patrick's family. Patrick would be a very necessary part of New Ecclon feeling like home.

Truly the most logical choice for the colony leadership team was Thatcher, a witty carpenter who had been working with Joshua on an expansion project for the Ecclon village housing area. Thatcher would bring his family. Joshua hated to let Thatcher go, because he had been Joshua's right-hand man in many of the technical aspects of Ecclonian village life. If anyone could find a solution to a problem, it was Thatcher. In fact, New Ecclon was originally Thatcher's idea. But, in typical Thatcher style, Thatcher had been training someone to take his place months before the council decided to colonize the valley. Thatcher always covered each angle and never lacked a well-thought out response to any situation.

These three families would go with Andrew. Others would follow, but these were the founding families. They would face and overcome many challenges together in the birthing of the new colony. Those challenges and the stories of each of these leaders will be told later. When the council met in Ecclon, Joshua opened the meeting by saying, "My sister, Piper, is not one to say, 'I told you so.' She would have every right to be, especially in this meeting. Eighteen months ago, she said we ought to consider connecting with Fort Follis in the valley and Benton by the River." She smiled and curtsied to return the honor to her brother.

With the New Ecclon team assembled, the four families and Piper left for the valley in early spring. Thatcher suggested an early spring crop planting so that the autumn harvest in New Ecclon would ensure that they survive its first winter – he thought of everything. Fueled by the adventurous excitement of this new town, Evan and Angela wasted no time visiting Fort Follis and Benton. And with the overwhelming love of Patrick's family, it wasn't long before New Ecclon had tripled in size. Piper made her regular, and sometimes random, trips up to Ecclon to report to Joshua what was going on down in the valley and brought back news to Andrew.

And thus New Ecclon was founded.

Another Perspective to Add to the Discussion

Throughout this book we will periodically come back to the story of Ecclon, adding perspective and discovering details of each leader's personality through their stories. It will serve as a parable to illustrate our look at the personalities of the Kingdom of God. Undoubtedly, there will be at least one person that you most identified with while reading. This will be a reference point, even before we delve into the depths of these personalities, as to which one you feel most connected to.

There have been several other authors who have done a fantastic job covering Ephesians 4 and what has been called "The Five Fold Ministry Offices". By no means is the goal in this work to contradict or diminish the studious explanations that they have offered. In fact, the goal in these pages is to complement and enhance the already robust understanding of the Five in a more personal context. The discussion on this topic is not complete or over.

If we took a cross-section of the teaching, preaching, digital and physical media in both the Christian and world markets, we would see one very dominant theme – identity. This issue of identity is at the core of humanity. The good news is that we are not in the dark; we are children of Light and know both where we came from and where we are going. The human struggle is not a matter of past or future, but of present identity.

This perspective has empowered individuals and communities to enjoy and cherish each other. As this perspective has been taught and understood, people have found themselves more confident in their unique contribution to the community, without the pressure to conform to a ministry model. Additionally, people have learned to relate to each other with more grace, excitement and celebration. Groups have found themselves better connected to each other inter-congregationally as well as to other congregations and even other streams of the Christian river. My prayer is that you will experience the freedom that I have seen from this revelation and understanding.

Apostles:
a Tribe of Pioneers and Stewards

The Parable of Ecclon: Andrew

Andrew and his twin brother Joshua grew up in Ecclon as it was growing into the village that it had become. Their father had founded the settlement when they were very young. Their family was the backbone of the community, and they loved Ecclon deeply. The terrain of the valley would be different from the mountainside, but in honor of his father, Andrew was dedicated to making New Ecclon a place that would have felt like home to his father.

Though Andrew was a great leader, he was not good at everything; he was, however, aware of his limitations. He knew that he had selected the best leaders to start the new colony. From the planning meetings with his brother to the actual transplanting of his family to the valley, Andrew was constantly seeing the big picture and delegating tasks to people. This was something that Andrew had learned from his father. People always felt empowered by Andrew because he believed in them and gave them room to succeed, but did not put pressure on them to not fail.

During the long trek down the mountain, across the valley, and eventually to the designated site of New Ecclon, Andrew was telling Evan and Angela stories about Ecclon under his father's leadership. They were so inspired that they began to quicken their pace, wanting to get settled soon and connect with the other villages in the valley. As the excited couple sped ahead, Thatcher came along side Andrew. Without an introduction, Thatcher started discussing the plan for the day, the weather projection, and his explanation of what needed to be done first in making preparations for construction. Andrew patiently listened, smiling the whole time at his friend's eccentric excitement. As soon as Andrew could get a word in, he agreed with Thatcher's plans and instructed him to pass along the plan to everyone prior to arrival in the valley.

As Thatcher hurried ahead to catch up with Evan and Angela, Andrew heard a rustling quickly approaching him from behind. It was his sister Piper. She looked concerned. Andrew stopped. "Andrew, Patrick is slowing down the back of the caravan. He is doing more talking than walking. At this pace, we won't make it by nightfall."

Andrew looked his wild-eyed sister in the eyes and calmed her down. "I will take care of it. Can you catch up with Thatcher, ask him about our plans, and let everyone know, please?" Piper knew what her big brother was doing, but she also knew that he was right to give her a task in order to get her focused on the goal. She smiled and said, "I can do that."

When Andrew reached what he thought would be the back of the caravan, he found Patrick's oldest son attempting to herd his siblings and other kids with a marching game. "Where is your father?"

"About 2 minutes behind us with mom. They are reminiscing and talking with your wife. I will get the rest of the kids caught up with Mr. Thatcher. Ms. Piper seemed a little stressed." Patrick's son was an observant and mature young man. Seeing the playful twinkle in the boy's eye, Andrew acknowledged his insight with a wink, a salute, and a fatherly punch to his shoulder.

Andrew found things exactly like Patrick's son had said. Without a word, Andrew got behind the strolling Patrick, put a hand on the middle of his back, and began to move him along a little faster. Andrew didn't want to disrupt the discussion; he rather liked Patrick's stories. Patrick didn't skip a beat in his storytelling, but quickened his pace as he realized what was happening. Andrew laughed as Patrick continued to tell stories despite the slow jog that the two couples were in.

By the time Andrew and company reached the kids, they were practically in a downhill sprint. Only barely maneuvering around the kids, Andrew yelled back to them, "First one to tackle Mr. Thatcher gets a candy bar!" Andrew was a fiercely competitive man, but more than anything he wanted to get everyone together and happy. He was a clever and thoughtful man.

Far before the sun touched the ridgeline, they had reached the site of New Ecclon. As Thatcher carried out the camp setup plan, Andrew walked around to ensure that everyone was accounted for and engaged in the task at hand. He bribed the kids with more candy in exchange for kindling and firewood.

They had made it. New Ecclon was really happening. Andrew felt excited, accomplished, and sober all at once. The next few months would test them, but Andrew was confident that this was going to be a great new chapter in their lives.

A Redefinition of "Apostle"

It is important to define the Five first by a biblical standard – how each term is used and what the actual word means – then, and only then, can we apply it to any other context. With that in mind, let us look at the way the New Testament handles the Apostle.

The word "apostle" is used less than 100 times in the Bible, which is not that many. In just Paul's letter to Rome, he mentions the Law almost as many times as apostles are mentioned in the entire Bible! In the gospels, Matthew and Mark each refer to Jesus' main 12 followers only once as "apostles." John only used the word "apostle" three times in his writings. He never used it in his gospel or his three pastoral letters, and in the Revelation two of the three were direct quotes of someone else speaking. The third reference was referring to the names of the 12 apostles' names being on the foundation of the New Jerusalem. Peter only uses the term to describe himself and the other 11 a couple of times. Jude uses it to refer to the 12. And though James was one of the 12, he never referred to himself as an apostle. Then the writer of the book of Hebrews refers to Jesus as "the Apostle and High Priest of our confession."

The bulk of the use of this word comes from the pens of Luke and Paul. Luke has half of the references in his gospel and the book of Acts, and they are almost exclusively used to describe the 12 disciples Jesus spent most of His time with. The remaining uses are from Paul. Luke travelled with Paul and wrote his two-part history of Christianity to defend Paul in Roman court. It is likely that Luke picked up on this terminology from Paul and the people he did his research with for his gospel and the book of Acts. Within Paul's writings, half of the uses of "apostle" are in reference to himself, specifically in his introductory greetings or in defending himself as an apostle. In the remaining few uses that are not referencing himself, Paul writes about the 12 apostles (seven times), twice uses "apostles" in the context of "false apostles" from whom he was defending the Corinthian church, and once he talks about two people who are apostles – one of which is a woman. Only three times does Paul use the term in reference to a general ministry, disconnected from specific people.

Why is this important?

First, consider that the entirety of the New Testament was written within the life span of those who witnessed the life, death and resurrection of Jesus. There was no time to establish a concept, expression or understanding of the way Christianity as an organized religion would work – especially compared to what we have developed in the last 2,000 years. Between persecution outside their congregations and heresies within, they did not have the leisure of developing these systems of thinking. They were mostly in survival mode.

However, the use of the term gives us insight into those who were considered apostles. It is clear that Jesus' twelve young men were apostles. Then it is important to evaluate the idea of an apostle with those young men as a primary example of what the essence of an apostle truly is, in any context or century.

Before we travel too far down this road, let me be clear that I am not an Ancient Languages scholar, but I did study Ancient Languages in college and it is a passion of mine to look at the parts of words to help me develop a dynamic personal understanding of the Biblical texts. With that being said, please take the following etymological breakdown of 'apostolos' and the other four Greek words with not just a grain of salt, but a whole salt lick.

The word *'apostolos'* is a combination of two words: *'apo'* and *'stello'*. *'Apo'* means, "separated," like the English word "apart." *'Stello'* means, "to cause to stand." So, an apostle is one who has been made to stand apart. Most lexicons say that it means something like "a sent one." This is why most translations have John 13:16 saying, "...the one sent..." or "...the messenger..." and not "...the apostle...", because it communicates the idea of the word more descriptively.

In ancient times, when an emperor wanted to start a new colony, he would send a small fleet of ships to the new settlement site. This fleet of ships carried everything needed to start the new colony and make it just like the capital city of the empire. There were political leaders, military personnel, educators, and anyone needed to bring the culture of the empire to this new place. The lead ship in the fleet was called 'the *apostolos*'. They were to be the team that was sent to stand apart from the empire, but still maintain the culture and essence of the empire.

This transfers over to the Biblical use of the term. Jesus, the Ultimate Apostle, is the first One sent from Heaven to the earth to create the culture of Heaven on the earth. Then He chose 12 disciples, like a rabbi does, and He sends them with the same mission that He was sent with – to make earth just like Heaven. The Emperor of the Universe will one day set foot on our dinky little planet and call it home, and Jesus was sent to create the race of the Saints who would prepare the earth for the coming of the Emperor. He started with the 12, who were taught the ways and mentalities of the Empire for 3 years with the First Apostle, and then they were sent to Jerusalem, Judea and Samaria, and then the ends of the earth to "establish the Kingdom" – prepare for the coming of the Emperor. Like the ancient colonizing teams, the whole focus of the '*apostolos* team' was to make the new colony as much like the empire as possible so that the emperor would feel at home when he came to visit. So it is for the apostles of God.

Looking at Paul's defense of his apostleship to the Corinthian church, we see what proofs he presented to be considered a true apostle of Jesus Christ, but for our purposes, it is important to see this on a less grandiose scale. In everyday life we act out of our core identity. This will manifest in any situation we find ourselves in. If you are an apostle, you will act like one in church, in relationships, in business, in every context that you encounter – in both major and minor ways. Later chapters will explain this for each of the Five.

Apostolic Mindsets and Attitudes

In order to really understand these apostles, let us look at the mentality and heart-motivations of a proto-typical apostle. Some of the examples and explanations of the Five will seem extreme, like caricatures that exaggerate the features. This is intentional. It will help us to identify with whomever we are most like. There are always outliers, counter-examples, and exceptions to the rules, but these are guidelines by which we can get a feel for the Five.

By the very nature of their commission and being sent, an apostle is mission-minded. They have been sent to do something, and they are stuck on that mission. Anything that gets in the way is a distraction, a waste of time that needs to be put aside. Peripheral details and seemingly unrelated concerns are inconsequential to an apostle.

At the very heart of an apostle is a love for the place they come from. It is easy for them to fight for the recreation of the culture they are representing, because they have a burning longing for their home. If they cannot be in the original atmosphere they were sent from, they will do everything in their power to establish that atmosphere where they are. They do not need to be told how to act or how to make their daily lives an expression of home. They carry "home" inside of themselves, and unconsciously bring the essence of home into every conversation and interaction. Every plan and every activity is obsessively pointing towards the recreation of that culture.

Since they are away from home, longing for the atmosphere of home, they tend to be builders. And every chance they get, they are looking to find like-minded people to spread out the borders of their expression of home. They are visionaries, big picture people, pioneers who build pockets of culture that can sustain the life they long for in the depths of their souls.

Strengths and Struggles

There are strengths and struggles for each of the Five. In order to rightly discern and become joined to the body, it is wise to be aware of both the strengths and struggles. This is not intended for introspection, self-exaltation, or dishonor. Rather, it is meant to help us celebrate each other's strengths and cover each other's struggles. It is a matter of honor.

Apostles have a solid obsession with the culture that they are recreating. They seem to only talk about that main thing, and conversations always come right back to the main thing. In a spiritual context, these are the people that are sometimes said to "be so heavenly minded that they are no earthly good." Their obsession can be infectious and it often rubs off on people, and that is the point, that is why God made them that way. They are leaders, focused on the goal. They are pioneers, determined to get just a little further on the path.

As a result, they can seem "myopic to the macro." They are stubborn and will fight tooth and nail for the accomplishment of the goal. It doesn't matter what the casualties are, the damages are necessary sacrifices for the cause. This can grate on those around them who have different callings, whether other apostles who are called to hold down the fort of another assignment or one of the other Four who have to deal with the details and hearts of those involved. They are not heartless; they are just very focused people who are being faithful to their assignment. They have to be stubborn in order to lead people in maintaining the culture they are recreating. Their extreme nature is necessary.

This tendency towards the extreme is actually a huge aide in the process of creating and carrying a community. They are able to make hard decisions easily because they have taken the emotions and man-pleasing out of the equation. They are able to have big personalities and be bigger than life so that people around them can identify with them and swim in the wake of what they are carrying. It is a gift to those that they lead for them to break up the ice for others to follow behind them in joining the vision trek. They carry the big vision of the community and can see how parts affect each other, where others can only see their small part.

Examples – Biblical, Historical, and Fictional

For each of the Five, we will take a look at some snapshot examples for each of the Five Tribes. We will look briefly at Biblical, historical, and fictional examples. These will not be perfect examples; unlike the preceding caricature explanations, these will serve more of a real life indication of each of the Five. These people are not necessarily what they are being used to illustrate, but we will look at how they acted as one of the Five in certain instances or ways.

Jesus had 12 apostles who are our primary examples of Biblical apostleship. They had a culture that they learned from Jesus. In Rabbinic training the teaching of a rabbi is called his "yoke." This was not simply the information that the rabbi taught, but it was really the way that the rabbi thought and acted towards people and situations. This is what Jesus was referring to when He said, "My yoke is easy and my burden is light" (Matthew 11:30). The disciples had caught the personal culture of Jesus, which He carried from His Father's Presence. As Jesus was sent to create that culture on the earth, so His disciples became apostles when they were sent out to recreate that same culture in Jerusalem, Judea, Samaria and the ends of the earth.

We can see this very obviously with Peter. When we look at Mark's gospel, which Peter essentially dictated to Mark, we see that Peter became Jesus 2.0 in his preaching, miracles, and style of relating. This shows up in the book of Acts and in Peter's letters. The personal culture of the Father was passed to Peter through Jesus, the Apostle and High Priest of our confession (Hebrews 3:1). He in turn passed that culture on to his disciples and we have received it through the generations of Christian history.

An interesting use of the word *'apostolos'* in the New Testament comes when Paul writes to the Philippian church. He writes to them what is basically an elaborate "Thank You" letter. In typical Pauline fashion, Paul cannot help but throw in some deep theological and incredibly profound revelations, but he is mostly writing to thank them for sending an offering for his needs while under house arrest. They sent this support in a very interesting way, with a man named Epaphroditus. This man brought the money from Philippi, but he stayed with Paul, cooked Paul's meals, and tended to Paul's needs. Most translations have Paul calling Epaphroditus a "messenger," but the word Paul uses is *'apostolos'*.

In our perspective of looking at the Apostle as one who is sent to recreate a culture, Epaphroditus fits the description perfectly. What better way to create a similar culture than to cook Philippian food and give a Philippian man to spend time with Paul? It makes no sense to call him a messenger; he wasn't primarily giving Paul a message, but he was certainly sent to bring the culture of a church family. A church family that started as a woman's prayer meeting when Paul baptized them in Acts 16. This is a perfect example of how an apostle does not have to lead a network of churches, move in unprecedented miraculous power or any other requirements that we think of. Epaphroditus simply brought money from his church, made meals, and hung out with Paul – and the most prolific writer in the New Testament, who used *'apostolos'* definitively, called him an Apostle.

In the Old Testament, there are a few examples of Apostles. Moses acted as an Apostle in that he defended the culture of the people of God, and throughout the entire trek through the wilderness he was the one setting the atmosphere and culture for the entire nation traversing a desert. When his leadership was challenged, it was by someone that I would also consider an Apostle, though not in a positive way. Korah tried to establish his own culture, and those who followed his apostolic leadership likewise shared in the punishment he accrued (Numbers 16). One of the great examples in Old Testament Scripture of an Apostle is King David. Specifically, when the Ark of the Covenant was being brought back to Israel, David was so stoked in his heart with excitement that he embarrassed his wife (2 Samuel 6). This created a culture of valuing the Presence of God, and as a result we see four decades of incessant worship. There were hundreds of very skilled musicians that supported this cultural value (1 Chronicles 13-16). He was Israel's Apostle, even when he was a little boy. His courage against a giant was infectious and gave courage to the rest of Saul's army (1 Samuel 17).

In a more contemporary Church context, John Wimber is an example of someone carrying an apostolic mandate. John Wimber is the founder of the Vineyard church movement. He was one of the first church leaders to make it a regular part of a church service to have people come up after a service for prayer if they were sick. John Wimber was an Apostle in that he knew that healing was part of Heaven's normal mode of operation and he doggedly pursued that reality in his life and the life of his churches. The culture of healing that most charismatic churches consider normal now is an inheritance that was established by John Wimber.

That is all well and good, but we need to really see a non-church example of this look at the Apostle. Look no further than the supermarket tabloids. Consider someone like Brad Pitt, Will Smith, Jennifer Anniston, or any other person you can think of that is a "trend setter." They are setting the culture of fashion and even activism. When Brad Pitt changed his hairstyle, others followed his example because of the apostolic anointing on his life. At some point there was a celebrity who realized that they had the power to shift culture. They didn't want to do it only in the realm of fashion, but wanted to make a difference, so they got involved in activism – clean water for African orphans, shoes for the poor children in India, the ending of sex trafficking. The media knows how to discern these "apostles," and they use them to promote the things that they want to promote. Whether that is a product, an idea, a political candidate or a new movie, there is a "sender" and an "apostle."

Let's refer back to our parable. Andrew is the Apostle in the story. His brother Joshua sent him, he loves Ecclon and wants to recreate that culture and feeling that his father had established. In each situation, Andrew was the leader. But he did not lord his leadership over others; he used it to put others in the right position to be most effective and benefit the greater body. He could see the big picture and recognized others' gifts and abilities, and he followed the example of his twin brother in his leadership style and structure. As we go through the other Four, we will see how important each part is and the analogy of valley colonies will become clearer and clearer.

Hopefully these examples have painted in some of the details of the picture of the Apostle. In later chapters we will see other aspects of the relationships between the Five. First we must get the broad brushstrokes of each of the Five and then fill in the details of them as a team – a family of personalities that need each other to be happy, fulfilled and successful in a community. Next we take a look at the Prophet.

Prophets:
a Tribe of Sculptors and Adjusters

The Parable of Ecclon: Piper

The third winter after the founding of New Ecclon was particularly cold and snowy on both mountain ranges. From its elevated perspective the whole valley and the opposite mountain range were visible. During their daily morning hikes, Piper and Joshua had seen a large collection of snow on the opposite peaks. From New Ecclon's perspective, even the brilliant and observant Thatcher would be unable to see the pending avalanche of late winter or the possible washout flooding of early spring. Piper had spent that winter up in Ecclon with Joshua. Piper was sent down to the valley to inform the people of the imminent danger the day after she and Joshua had noticed the threat to the valley.

On her way down the mountain, Piper took a new trail North to Fort Follis to let them know what was coming in just a couple of months. The people of Fort Follis had always envied the Ecclonians. All they knew of them was that their village was growing and happy, and whenever someone went to investigate, they rarely came back. They also resented the New Ecclonians for the same reasons and because the crops were so much healthier around New Ecclon. So when Ecclon's princess came to help them, they would not receive her. They called her arrogant and misinformed. Their leader said, "Our valley has never seen an avalanche or a washout flood in the many decades my family has stewarded it – many years before your father settled on the mountainside. What makes Ecclon think it knows better than Fort Follis and its long history in the valley?"

Not wanting to waste time with people who weren't listening to her, Piper turned south to New Ecclon. Immediately upon her arrival, the Five leaders of New Ecclon gathered in Andrew's house.

Piper gave the warning about what was coming. Patrick quickly spoke up, "We cannot tell the others about this problem; it will bring panic. But if we come up with a plan to help save the rest of the valley, everyone will gladly prepare to help our brothers to the North in Fort Follis and our river brothers in Benton. I'm sorry that they did not listen to you, Piper. Maybe we can speak with them together."

Piper looked to her brother Andrew for permission to go back to Fort Follis with Patrick. The urgency still hung in her heart, but the message had been delivered to her people. Now she could take patient Patrick with her to see if they could reach their neighbors. Before leaving, Piper sat down with Thatcher and explained to him what she saw on the mountain. From her description, Thatcher would be able to make a plan for the possible catastrophes.

As Piper was leaving, she quickly mentioned to Andrew that Benton by the river would be in the most danger from a flood. Andrew had already thought of that and Thatcher had already made a plan for that contingency. Immediately, Evan and Angela volunteered to go down to Benton to talk to the many friends they had made there over the past year. Content that her message was in the hands of very capable people, Piper set out to Fort Follis with Patrick.

Just as suspected, the warning was better received from Patrick. He had a way of appealing to them in a manner that was more palatable than Piper had been. Piper was able to better explain what was going on once Patrick had opened up the door for her. Fort Follis would be saved after all. Thatcher would partner with the engineers in Fort Follis to prepare for either disaster.

Relieved that her voice had been heard and crisis would be averted, Piper went back to New Ecclon to see if Andrew had anything he wanted to tell Joshua, or if there was anything else she could do. The burden was off of her shoulders and Piper was ready to move on to the next assignments.

A Redefinition of "Prophet"

The word used in the New Testament for Prophet comes from two words: *'pro'*, meaning, "before", and *'phemi'*, meaning, "to declare." A prophet is someone who declares an event before it happens. Most specifically, the Biblical prophets were those that were sent by God to declare His coming – in the Old Testament declaring the coming of Jesus, and in the New Covenant prophets declare His return. But the declaration is not a transfer of information, a cosmic public service announcement; the declaration of a prophet has purpose. The main purpose is to alert the hearers that the coming event requires a change. Preparation needs to be done and many times the prophet is the one who carries a blueprint of what needs to change.

Like the Apostle, the focus of the Prophet is to prepare for the Emperor's coming. The difference is that the Prophet is generally sent to an already established entity – person or community – that is already oriented towards the Empire. The Apostle has already been sent, has started to recreate the culture of the Empire, and is empowering those in the community to live in the transplanted cultural norms that the Apostle left the Empire with in his heart. The Prophet is the one sent to make additional arrangements for the Emperor. They come to adjust, shift, and sculpt the culture of the Apostle's community to best suit the desires of the Emperor.

The Old Testament Scriptures almost always speak of a Prophet as a descriptive title for someone who was sent by God with a message of change for a nation – mostly Israel, but other nations as well. Matthew's gospel uses the term 'prophet' more than any other New Testament book, 30 of those 36 times refer to those who came before Jesus whose lives pointed to and prepared the world for the coming of Jesus. These men were friends of God, who shifted and sculpted the cultural beliefs and behaviors of nations to make way for the Emperor's Son. James, Jesus' half-brother, gives a very succinct and simple definition for the Old Testament prophets. James said they were the ones "who spoke in the name of the Lord" (James 5:10). Then Peter (likely on the very next page of your Bible after James' definition) gives a great description of the lives of the Old Testament prophets. Peter wrote that the Old Testament prophets made careful searches and inquiries about the coming of the Lord Jesus (1 Peter 1:10). They prophesied concerning the timing and the nature of who He is and what He would do. He echoed Paul's sentiment in Ephesians 4 that the prophets knew that they were sent to serve others and prepare the way in people's hearts for Christ's coming.

In one of His five major sermons recorded in Matthew's gospel, Jesus makes a crucial statement about honoring a prophet. He says that if we recognize and honor a prophet as a prophet, then we get the impartation or "reward" that the prophet carries as a part of their life (Matthew 10:41). In a later sermon Jesus is confronting the cultural leaders of that time and He says that He is going to send prophets to them, which He says will be rejected and even killed (Matthew 23:34). Apparently Jesus, being a Prophet Himself, could foresee that these leaders would not pass the test of receiving His prophets. But the challenge stands for us: will we recognize and honor those who God sends to us? The first step is to have an understanding of what to look for. In other words, how do the New Testament Scriptures define a prophet so that we know how to receive His emissaries rightly?

In doctor Luke's historical defense of the early Church, a man named Agabus is called a prophet (Acts 21:10). We read that he predicted that a famine would come, which did happen during the reign of Claudius. As a response, the believers in Antioch responded by collecting provision for the people who would be affected by the famine. Here we see Agabus giving a new direction for the finances of his church (Acts 11). Ten chapters later we read about Agabus again prophesying, this time warning Paul of impending persecution in Jerusalem for him. Again, he was correct. And though he was right, his application of this warning was apparently wrong; Paul did not avoid the danger but embraced it, and was certainly more prepared for what was about to happen as a result.

Also in the book of Acts, Luke mentions a false prophet named Bar-Jesus. This man, also called Elymas, was trying to persuade the proconsul to avoid and reject Paul and Barnabas. Paul, however, performed a sign to expose Elymas as a false prophet, thereby amazing and helping the proconsul to avoid

Elymas' deception (Acts 13). In Acts 21 there is a quick mention of Philip's daughters who were all called prophetesses. And though the word "prophet" is not used in Acts 15, the elders and leaders in Jerusalem function in a prophetic way when they hear from the Lord and write a letter explaining that Christian believers need not embrace the Jewish laws first in order to enter the Kingdom. This adjusted and sculpted the culture of Christianity in a very pivotal way and in an extremely critical time in the development of Church history.

For our intents and purposes, think of a Prophet as one whose main focus in all that they say and do is to tweak the world around them. A Prophet has foresight and concern for the end result and has a passion to see the current systems and culture produce an adequate welcome for an emperor when he arrives.

Prophetic Mindsets and Attitudes

The creation of the marathon is a fascinating story from the ancient world. It illustrates the passion of the Prophet very well. The simplified crux of the story is that a messenger's main goal is the delivery of the message, not their own comfort or purpose or livelihood. After a battle in the city of Marathon, a young messenger ran 40,000 meters to Athens in order to report of the victory in Marathon. By the time Pheidippides got to Athens, he only had enough strength to say, "Niki." – which means "victory" – and then fell dead from exhaustion. In the same way, a Prophet's soul reverberates with the message they are carrying. Their message is the most important thing and they must deliver it. Why? Because it is in their nature; just as a baker bakes, a messenger gives a message.

The initial push of a Prophet is their message-mindedness. But once a Prophet has given their message, it is their responsibility to follow through with it. This comes innately, for the most part, to Prophets because their message is in their pulse and they cannot escape it simply by delivering a message. Similar to the Apostle, who not only pioneers a culture but is entrusted with the task of maintaining that culture, the Prophet is transformation oriented. They will stick around until the necessary tweaks are implemented or at least they are confident that there is sufficient oversight to ensure that the transformation will be accomplished.

The Prophet doesn't think that the culture they are sent to transform is bad. They are simply burning with the message of transformation. More than anything, Prophets have an epic advent at their heart – the coming of the Emperor. Their mission is to manifest the necessary preparations so that the Emperor is pleased with the colony. The accusation could be made that they are afraid of the Emperor, but that is not true. At the very heart of the Prophet is a love for the Emperor and a desire to give Him what He deserves. So adjustments *must* be made.

Whether an all new direction or a slight correction to a minor policy or mentality, the Prophet is an adjuster. The Prophet's heart is throbbing with one question from which their entire value system is birthed: what else can make things a better landing place for what is coming?

Strengths and Struggles

Each of the Five has their perks and their limitations. One of the many strengths of the Prophet is their fresh revelations and perspectives. They are a breath of fresh air and carry a new perspective. In a Church context, this comes as dynamic teachings and exciting insight into next steps for a community of faith. In other settings, the Prophet seems to always be on the cutting edge of trends and opportunities. This freshness, excitement and foresight ensure that a community is more like a river than a swamp – things are always moving. Instead of cisterns that gather stagnant water, Prophets keep things flowing in and going out.

Another very beneficial aspect to having an active and empowered Prophet in your life is that they are generally a failsafe against major future problems. Prophets bring the future into the present. They see where things are going and help to steer the community, and even individuals, away from potentially harmful or detrimental future collisions. Imagine being in a hostile situation, trying to solve a Rubik's Cube. Your attention would be split between your safety and the task at hand. But with a watchman, you can confidently devote your attention to the Rubik's Cube while they are looking for and protecting you from assailants. This is what a Prophet does; they allow those in the community to stay on task and plow hard, knowing that they are not going to get blind-sided by an unseen enemy.

Now, if we do not discern a Prophet and appreciate them for who they are and what they do best, we will think they are negative people. It is easy to misinterpret the incessant tweaking and adjusting as micromanaging, nitpicking, or disapproval. And Prophets that have not been celebrated for their foresight, otherworldly wisdom, and understanding will be judged to be micromanagers and nitpickers, and they will be accused of being judgmental. The longer someone is told they are something, the more likely it is that they will begin to agree with the accusation. Too many Prophets, inside and outside the Church context, have taken on the nature of these accusations. They become judgmental and disapproving of everything they see that they know won't pan out. Then the Prophet's discernment will become endorsed in their own minds by the immanent failure that people ignored because of the attitude or personality of the Prophet.

This becomes a vicious cycle. External rejection from personality conflict or immaturity conflicts with a Prophet's internal confirmation of their true identity. The conflict is exacerbated when the Prophet is proven to have been right in the message that they were rejected over. So then, bucking against the rejection and still trying to contribute to the community the way they are meant to, Prophets try again to make an adjustment. They site their previous correct discernment and are labeled "arrogant" for tooting their own horn.

These conflicts happen primarily in an immature prophetic culture, with underdeveloped Prophets. Partnering with a Pastor, the heart of the Prophet will be cared for and appreciated, but the key to avoiding these kinds of snafus is to honor and receive people for who they are and evaluate their limitations with love and patience.

Examples – Biblical, Historical, and Fictional

The Bible is chock full of examples of Prophets, both in the spiritual office and in the sense of a personality Tribe. Chief among the examples is no less than Jesus Himself. Jesus, sent by the Emperor of Existence – His very own Father – came to earth to prepare both humanity and creation for the permanent habitation of God. In the book of the Revelation, we see that the ultimate focus of the End of Days is not the Second Coming of Jesus, but the relocation of the abode of the Ancient of Days. Jesus came preaching new perspectives on the Law, on God's nature and character, and on life in general to a generation that would begin the preparations for His Father's Kingdom.

While Jesus made adjustments to understanding the Law in sermons like Matthew 5-7 (known by most as "the Sermon on the Mount"), before He came as a man, He sent others to prepare for His own coming. He sent Jonah to proclaim correction to an extremely insane nation, and though Jonah had a poor attitude, he still brought His message to Nineveh and served as a prophetic sign of Jesus that Jesus pointed to – talk about redemption of a mistake!

It is common for the life of a Prophet to be a message in and of itself. Not only did God turn Jonah's life into a sign (Matthew 12:39 and Luke 11:29), sometimes He actually called people to embody the message. Hosea was a prophet who was so yielded to the message he carried that he was willing to marry a prostitute. Gomer would continue in her promiscuity and Jonah would faithfully declare what God was saying by how he related to his wife. Many Prophets in my life have done similar things that I thought were absolute insanity. They were judged, but in the end, their lives were a bullhorn declaration of the heart of Jesus for those with eyes to see and ears to hear.

As with all of the Five (and this should go without saying) there is no gender specificity in being a Prophet. Mary acted as a Prophet. After Jesus had resurrected but not yet ascended to the Father to finish His job, she went and declared to the disciples that Jesus was raised from the dead. She opened up the whole community, which was presently in a depression party after their

Rabbi apparently hadn't turned out to be the Messiah (at least not as they assumed He would).

In Church history, there have been many Prophets who have come with adjustments to the Church's mentality towards God. Martin Luther was confronted with the true power of Faith. From Luther's life we had a reformation, a transformation of global proportions to the Church.

And hundreds of years later, a man would be named after Luther who would be a Prophet to America. Martin Luther King Jr. took a message of civil rights and equality to America. Regardless of whether his message was from God or not (which most would agree that it was), King's life impacted one of the most powerful nations in history at a pivotal point in its development. He helped to change the way people thought. He helped the United States avoid some major pitfalls that would inevitably destroy it from its application of foundational American values of freedom.

From our opening parable of Ecclon, Piper was the Prophet. She lived with both her brothers, communicating with both what was happening with the other – serving not just as a Prophet, but also as an intercessor of sorts. Because of her perspective, she was able to see what would happen in the Spring. She was rejected by one town, as many Prophets have been when trying to help.

Go back and reread the parable, you will see it more clearly, and then we will move on to the Evangelist.

Evangelists: a Tribe of Promoters and Gatherers

The Parable of Ecclon: Evan and Angela

When Evan and Angela were called to the meeting at Andrew's house, they had just gotten back from a trip in Benton. The friends that they had made in Benton were precious to them. So the news of a pending flood that could possibly destroy Benton was devastating. They were more than happy to head back down to Benton and extend Joshua's invitation to join New Ecclon on the lower plateau.

Truth be told, Evan and Angela had been inviting Bentonians every time they visited. They loved New Ecclon as much as they had loved Ecclon, and they wanted everyone to experience the vibrant community that had developed there. Evan and Angela met with Andrew and Thatcher before leaving to be sure that they understood exactly what was going on, and to clarify what New Ecclon could do for the Benton residents with the dangerous end of winter quickly approaching.

Though the urgency of Piper's message compelled them, Evan and Angela hiked south with smiles on their faces and a skip in their step. They were never good at being somber. They found the joy and excitement in everything. When they arrived in Benton they were greeted warmly.

One of the Benton residents asked why they were back so soon, Evan shook himself and said, "Oh yes! I was so glad to see you again, I almost forgot. There is a huge snow build up beyond Fort Follis that could destroy all three of our villages. I need to talk to your leaders. Andrew and Thatcher have a plan that will work, but we have to start now. Of course, you could all just move to

New Ecclon." Everyone smiled at Evan's bold proposition – it wasn't the first time he had made this suggestion.

The Benton leaders trusted Evan and Angela. But this was a big deal. They needed to decide on a plan of action. Angela suggested that they send an engineer back to New Ecclon to get the full picture and plan from Thatcher. Just as they agreed to this, Thatcher walked into the room. "No need, I'm here."

After a thorough yet succinct explanation from Thatcher, the Benton leaders were split. Some were willing to move to the plateau and others were unwilling to leave their homes. Evan and Angela did their best to try to sway the others despite the obvious reality that Benton could not be abandoned. Over the following days, Evan and Angela would stick around to help pack up the belongings of the Benton families that were going to relocate. The day that the relocation caravan was to head North to New Ecclon and the plateau, Thatcher and Evan and Angela left extra early to reach New Ecclon. They needed to prepare the village for a sudden influx of residents. There was much that would need to change to accommodate their river friends.

A Re-definition of "Evangelist"

At this point, let me reiterate that by no means am I attempting to give the definition of each of the Five. Note the subtitle of this book; this is an answer to the Christian identity crisis. The intention of this book is not to "give the real definition that has been lost for ages and generations, but has been divinely revealed to an unsuspecting young man from Michigan". Rather, I am sharing a perspective that can help people understand, honor and appreciate those around us. That being said, let's redefine "evangelist" for our purposes.

The word "evangelist" comes from the Greek word '*euangelistes*', which comes from two root words: '*eu*', meaning "good," and '*angelia*', meaning "message."

This is why the Gospel is many times called "the Good News"; it isn't just because it is, in fact, great news. So those who gave most of their time and energy, and who were gifted and called by God, to tell people this Great News of salvation were called "good news-ers" – Evangelists. At the most basic level, an Evangelist is the embodiment of a Good Message.

In a very real sense, an Evangelist is charged with the job of *being* the message that they carry. They are the marketers, the promoters, and the ones who gather others to that which they are excited about. Recently I was listening to sports radio. A fairly new NFL cornerback was being interviewed by ESPN at a sports bar. When the interviewer asked him why he comes in each week for the radio show wearing a different NBA team's hat each week, the football player said, "Well, I can't wear any of the other NFL team's hat." What we are excited about will come out in what we talk about, what we wear, and how we spend our time and resources. Clearly this football player was not super excited about being a billboard for his team more than he had to be – I can't say I blame him.

In noun form, 'evangelist' is only used three times in the New Testament. The first time is in Acts 21 to describe Philip. Then there is the passage in Ephesians 4 upon which this entire book is based. The third place is again from Paul, writing to his spiritual son, encouraging him to do the work of an evangelist while leading the church in Ephesus (2 Timothy 4). This third reference is important for us to understand because Timothy is functioning in an apostolic role. Paul sent Timothy to take care of eldership and other administrative leadership issues, even though Timothy is much more of a Pastor in his heart and Tribe. Yet Paul is still urging him to do the work of an evangelist. No matter what your role or your calling, you can always do what is needed in another position.

Now, this still leaves the 50+ primary uses of this word as a verb in the New Testament. Many of these references are translated in most versions of the Bible as "preach the Gospel." It is a fascinating study to look at who does the preaching or evangelizing. God evangelized the Old Covenant prophets (Revelation 10). Gabriel evangelized a group of night watch shepherds (Luke 2). John the Baptizer (Luke 3), Jesus Himself and His young adult ministry team (the disciples) and even Paul throughout the book of Acts each evangelized. It is apparent that to a certain extent, anyone can do the evangelizing.

In every case, there is a definite thread that runs through each "good news-er" – they are presenting an invitation to the targets of their evangelizing. Whether it is the apostles in the book of Acts being scattered to the edges of the Middle East and Mediterranean regions or Paul searching for fresh ears to hear the Good News, as Evangelists they were essentially calling people to change the way they lived. This is what Evangelists do, they challenge, they promote, and they gather.

An Evangelist is that person in your community that is always bringing new people to parties and events. They are a good example of a community, so they are always inspiring others to come and check out this community that so greatly impacted their lives. People look at Evangelists and think, "Well, if they are *that* excited about it, it must be worth looking into." Evangelists aren't just good messengers, carrying a good message – they *are* the message.

Evangelistic Mindsets and Attitudes

Have you ever worked at a company that gave their employees free merchandise? Companies do this not just for the sake of making the employees feel like they are getting a good deal by working at a place that gives them free things *and a paycheck.* They do it for two much more crucial reasons for the advancement of their company.

First, they do it for free advertising. In particular, clothing brands require their workers to wear only their brand while working. This is only logical while they work, but the result is that each season the employees get another addition to their wardrobe. Inevitably, these employees will have to wear these clothes even when they aren't at work – by sheer volume overload in their closet alone. It isn't like they give the clothes back after they quit, so that is basically free advertising for as long as those clothes stay in circulation and style.

Secondly, and more subconsciously, they do it to make it easy for the employees to know the product and develop a positive opinion of the brand. The more experience someone has with the product they are selling, the more affective they can become in selling it. It is generally my policy that if I am at a new restaurant and don't know what to get, I will ask the waiter what they suggest. I cannot tell you how many times I have simply gone with what they suggested simply because they said it was their favorite, not because I actually wanted what they suggested. Why? They had experienced something and I wanted the same experience, assuming that they had tried everything else.

In the same way, Evangelists have it built into their nature to make sure that others know about what they have experienced. They are natural salesmen or marketers, and are able to convince you that you should at least give this thing a chance. Now, they do not do it consciously all the time. Most of the time it is simply an overflow of who they are, just like a Prophet sculpts and adjusts their surroundings without trying. Evangelists do not wake up in the morning and think, "How can I coerce people into enjoying everything that I enjoy today?" It is completely natural. In every situation they are excited to help others experience what they have recently experienced.

The human soul has been described as being made up of the Mind, the Will and the Emotions; it is the Will that Evangelists target. Inspiration. That is what drives an Evangelist in the core of their being. This inspiration happens both within the community and outside the community that the Evangelist is connected to. From within, the Evangelist lives in such a way that they inspire the rest of the community to better represent the community. Not always directly, but in some way the cry of the Evangelist's life is, "change the way you are living so that we look really good to outsiders. What we have is unique and valuable, let's bring in others to experience it with us!" Outside of the community, Evangelists inspire strangers to become friends, outsiders to become vitally connected, and cynics to become users.

An Evangelist is the Headline of the Good News incarnated. But they are not at all passive in manifesting the nature of their message. They have legs and they use them, and everywhere they go is just another pulpit to share their excitement about their message and how it has changed their lives.

Strengths and Struggles

When a community has a functioning and thriving Evangelist or two, there is never a lack of fun or excitement. Evangelists are dynamic and challenge the community to improve itself and become the most dynamic, full version of itself that it can become. Evangelists have incredible stories and tend to regularly have something inspirational happening to them. They enjoy interacting with people and being the center of attention. They live in the moment and are not actually thinking about themselves while getting attention. Rather, they are just so caught up in the latest, most exhilarating aspect of life around them, that they are drawing attention to themselves to point them to something else. It isn't about them.

Strictly in terms of their function in a community, Evangelists are the essential ingredients for ensuring that a community continues to be alive and growing. By being excited about what is stirring in a community, Evangelists are incessantly bringing new people in to experience the stirring for themselves. This generates more excitement and more energy in those already invested in the community, and thereby more reasons to be excited. They bring life, maintain life, and renew life.

With this obsession with fun, energy, and excitement, it can be hard to get an Evangelist rolling in a stagnant community. If there is nothing that, in their eyes, is worthy of a genuine enthusiasm, it will be difficult to motivate them toward gathering people or promoting the community. And even when something exciting is happening, an Evangelist can tend to become bored with "the same old life as usual." Even if the current 'life as usual' is the 'exciting future' of the past, once it becomes routine, disinterest can set in, and they can get disconnected.

It becomes the responsibility of the leaders of a community to maintain motivation in the lives of Evangelists. This is not all that difficult, because they are prone to excitement. Any slight morsel of something new on the horizon will do. But this requires Apostles and Prophets and other leaders to keep the Evangelists in the loop. As long as leaders are aware of the positive and negative tendencies of those they are leading, they can structure the way they lead so as to maximize the benefits and avoid the pitfalls. In later chapters we will discuss how to relate between each of the Five most affectively. Honoring the others will bring out their strengths.

Examples – Biblical, Historical, and Fictional

Another way to look at the essence of an Evangelist is that they live the culture of a community outside of that community and as a result draw people into that community. As with everything, Jesus is the ultimate example of an Evangelist. He lived the culture of Heaven when He came to earth, and that drew people into desiring that Kingdom to expand as they entered into it. John the Revelator sees Him standing in Heaven, calling to us saying, "Come up here" (Revelation 11:12). In typical Evangelist fashion, Jesus is marketing the Kingdom and giving His inspired hearers an ultimatum and an invitation – "Repent...come follow Me."

Joseph, the grandson of Abraham, functioned as an Evangelist in that he embodied the blessing, favor, and heritage-culture of Grandpa Abe as he circuitously stepped into authority in Egypt. Abraham's business anointing and encounter lifestyle passed down to his descendants. When Joseph was in Egypt, he accessed that familial culture, brought it into the present, and saved millions of people – including his brothers who had betrayed and rejected him the last time he saw them.

In a similar scenario, Daniel worked for one of the most demonized rulers in the history of the world. Yet he lived out the supernatural culture of the Kingdom and was regarded as a master sage-magician, interpreted a pagan king's dream, and in the end, an entire nation was instructed by that king to worship Daniel's God. His influence in the satanic supernatural culture inundated a whole people group with the Divine blessing of friendship with God.

There were two "Philips" in the New Testament. Of course there was the Philip of Acts 8, who is called an Evangelist. But there was another Philip in John 1. The second Philip only knew Jesus for a matter of days, yet he tracked down Nathanael and convincingly informed him that he had found the Messiah. When Nathanael challenged Philip's assertion, Philip's confident "come and see" was enough to bring Nathanael into the Messianic Ministry Team.

For those old enough to remember David Robinson, the Admiral is remembered as one of the great examples of a Christian professional athlete. David Robinson is an NBA Hall of Famer who represented Christ in a realm of society not known for its strong moral compass in a time when there were multiple counterexamples to point at. Robinson was well known for praying before games, even connecting with players on other teams who were Christians to encourage them in their faith, as well as consistently demonstrating his devotion to Jesus in charitable giving and the creation of businesses that were overtly Christian in their values. Robinson took Kingdom values and the culture of faith and Christian character into the professional sports world. Did he do traditional "evangelism" by leading other players to the Lord? Sure. But he was an Evangelist in that he embodied the message that you do not have to be an immoral, wild, or otherwise worldly person to be successful in that realm of society.

In the parable of Ecclon, Evan and Angela are the Evangelists. It is easy to see. They were the fun ones, the ones who connected with other villages, and the ones who came back to New Ecclon to prepare for the Benton families that were joining them on the plateau. If you want to go back a few pages and re-read the parable, feel free. If not, let's move on to the Pastor.

Pastors:
a Tribe of Inspirers and Protectors

The Parable of Ecclon: Patrick

After hearing about the potential danger in the valley, Patrick switched gears. He put aside the slow-walking, reminiscing man that everyone saw on the path from Ecclon all those years ago. Patrick, who was usually fairly disinterested in details and plans, instantly became the most informed person in New Ecclon. His concern for the people of Fort Follis and Benton consumed him.

Patrick accompanied Piper back to Fort Follis in hopes that they would be saved. Patrick was not a soft-spoken man, but when he spoke with people, they could sense the tenderness in his heart towards them. This was the main factor in his success with the leaders of Fort Follis. Where Piper had been unable to get through to them, Patrick appealed to the safety of their children. As he spoke, it sounded to them as though Patrick was as emotionally invested as a grandfather would be in the safety and future of his grandchildren.

Having reached the leaders in Fort Follis with Piper's message, Patrick released her back to New Ecclon with a message for Andrew. Patrick, however, remained a couple more days in Fort Follis. He took the time to meet with all of the heads of families. Patrick wanted to be sure that everyone knew what was going on, that there was a good plan to take care of everyone, and that they were welcome to move south to New Ecclon if they still felt unsafe in Fort Follis.

There was a small group of men and their families that would go with Patrick back to New Ecclon. They would settle just north of the lower plateau, so that they could be closer to Fort

Follis. From there they could be part of the preparation team for both villages, while still ensuring that their families were shielded from danger. Patrick made sure that the Fort Follis leadership was comfortable with the plans and then led the group south to New Ecclon.

The moment Patrick and his entourage arrived in New Ecclon, Patrick was busy getting them settled and connected to the rest of the village. That first night, Patrick and his wife hosted a village-wide party to welcome their new friends to the New Ecclon family. Evan, Angela, and Thatcher walked into the party just as it was winding down. They were fresh off the trail from Benton and though it was late, Thatcher requested an immediate meeting with of the Five leaders.

Dragging himself away from the end of the party, Patrick was the last one to the meeting. Thatcher updated everyone on Benton and the plan for preparation down south. The last bit of information that Thatcher gave was the number of families that would be joining New Ecclon from Benton. Everyone was shocked at the thought of how much work the coming weeks would require to nearly double the size of New Ecclon. Oblivious to the reaction of the others, Patrick exclaimed, "You know what this means? Another village party tomorrow night!"

Andrew smiled at Patrick, winked at the others, and dismissed the meeting.

A Re-definition of "Pastor"

What we call a "pastor" in the Western church is not what a pastor is meant to be. The way most of the Western church thinks about a "pastor" is as the main speaker at church services and the primary decision maker. This is not what a true pastor is, and it certainly does not reflect the understanding of Pastor as a personality Tribe. There are multiple words in the Old and New Testaments that build a definition of a Pastor, and they all point to one who cares for and is focused on the heart and wellbeing of those they are leading – not an organization helmsman or a community's chief communicator.

Steps down from soapbox

The word used in Ephesians 4 that most translation have as "pastor" is primarily used to describe shepherds. Not in a metaphorical sense, but in a very ordinary sense – as in the herder of sheep. In fact, a large chunk of the uses of this word *'poimen'* are used to describe Jesus' heart towards people, compassion for "sheep without a Shepherd"(Matthew 9:36). And that is the heart behind true Pastors; they care about the hearts of the community.

But two questions arise: How did we make the jump from the Shepherd-Pastor to the CEO-Pastor? And if this word is only used once to describe a church leader, how did it become the prominent position in our churches? The answer to both comes in doing some verse linking and a deep dive into the life of the Near East shepherd.

Strong's Concordance explains it this way: "A shepherd in the Near East was responsible for watching out for enemies trying to attack the sheep, defending the sheep from attackers, healing the wounded or sick sheep, finding and saving lost or trapped sheep, loving them, and sharing their lives, and earning their trust." In a more modern look, the shepherd was the sniper protecting the valuable assets of a master or owner. Not just a protector, but also one who gives their life to care for needs of the sheep. Shepherds were snipers and medics and councilors, all wrapped up in one package.

After Paul had spent three years in Ephesus, planting and developing a church, he gathered the "elders" together and addressed them in a farewell speech that Luke recorded in Acts 20. This speech sheds some light on biblical shepherding and pastorship.

The word used in verse 17 for "elders" is the word that the "Presbyterian" church is named after. It essentially just means, "older people." The terms "presbyter," "elder" and "bishop" are used interchangeably in the New Testament; however, each of these terms means a more mature believer that others look to for wisdom and leadership. In a Jewish sense, the elders were those in the Sanhedrin. They were generally elderly and therefore had more experience – they possessed the wisdom necessary to make rulings and judgments.

It is fascinating how vital this one speech is in constructing a Scriptural understanding of a Pastor. Though Luke says that Paul called together the *'presbyteros'* (verse 17), when Paul speaks to them he uses the language of the *'poimen'* to exhort them to "guard the flock" and "shepherd the Church which He purchased" (verse 28). But even more fascinating is that Paul neither calls them *'poimen'* nor *'presbyteros'*, he calls them "overseers". The Greek word he uses is *'episkopos'* – after which the "Episcopalian" church derives its name.

This word tends to be Paul's preferred term in his apostolic epistles when referring to a church leader who cares for the people. I want to clarify what I mean by "apostolic epistles." Paul's practice was to start a church by speaking to the Jews of a city first, if there were any, and then seeing if there were Gentiles who would receive Jesus. Once there was a growing group, like in Ephesus, he would spend time discipling the believers. Eventually he would train and appoint leaders. These leaders were called "elders" and "deacons." The elders were primarily in charge of the spiritual and emotional state of the flock – as we have discussed so far. Deacons were the practical leaders, the admin team who took care of details that would otherwise keep the elders from leading well. The word for them was *'diakonos'*, which we simply transliterated to get "deacon." It comes from a word used in the New Testament that meant, "to run an errand."

After establishing elders and deacons, Paul would move on to another city or region and send back epistles – a fancy shmancy seminary word for "letter." These letters are "apostolic," not simply because they are written by an apostle, but because of the letters' nature and purpose. They were intended to address problems, redirect focus, and illuminate important aspects of the state of the Church – they helped to maintain the culture, exactly what an Apostle does. We see this in the Corinthian letters, especially. There were problems he was dealing with, responding to concerns and reports from members of the First Church of Corinth (or whatever they decided to put on the sign out front), and helping steer the church – at times unsuccessfully. When he was not successful he would send an apostolic delegate, like Timothy or Titus, to be his representative.

We see that Paul was very concerned with who the overseers, elders, and deacons were in his letters to Timothy and Titus. With Titus, Paul's hard-nosed "git-er-dun" apostolic delegate to Crete, we see that Paul had particular characteristics that he wanted the Cretan overseers to have. However, Timothy, Paul's tender-hearted apostolic delegate and spiritual son, Paul sent him to Ephesus to deal with some hard leadership restructuring – something that Titus would have been more gifted for, in my opinion. But Paul gave a similar list of characteristics for overseers to Timothy, though slightly modified for the Ephesians' situation. Timothy also helped Paul write to the elders and deacons in Philippi, so apparently he had enough understanding of what was important – having been discipled by Paul.

Back to the "overseer," after that apostolic epistle rabbit trail.

"Overseer" is a perfect translation for the word *'episkopos'*. It breaks down into two root words: *'epi'* and *'skopos'*. *'Epi'* is the word we get the prefix for words like "epicenter," the very heart and center of a region or explosion. And a *'skopos'* is a watchman or observer, but is the word we get our English word "skeptic" from. This lines up with what we saw Strong's Concordance says about the shepherd. An overseer, or Pastor, is the one who stands in the middle of the flock, being skeptical of anything that approaches. Consequently, when Peter refers to Jesus as "the Shepherd and Guardian of our souls," the words he uses are *'poimen'* and *'episkopos'* (1 Peter 2:25).

Just in case you are not yet convinced that a Pastor is a shepherd, below are a few Old Testament passages that provide more of a backdrop for understanding the Pastors of the New Testament.

Able, a prophetic picture of Jesus in the shedding of his blood that cried out from the ground to God, was a shepherd (Genesis 4:2). The Hebrew word is *'ra'ah'*. Jacob called God his "Shepherd of his life" (Genesis 48:15) and when prophesying over his children he called Him "the Shepherd and Rock of Israel"

(Genesis 49:24). Then David was called to a meeting with Israel's leaders at Hebron, they reminded him that he was called by God to "shepherd" Israel, though they simply called Saul's leadership "ruling" (2 Samuel 5:2) – this dichotomy of leadership style is notable. David saw God not as a distant deity, but as his Shepherd as we read in Psalm 23, and he passed this view of God to his son. Solomon called God "the One Shepherd" in Ecclesiastes 12:11 and in the Song of Songs it is remarkable how throughout the story of the romance story, the Man is seen near sheep – this reveals the close relationship of the sheep and shepherd.

The young prophet Jeremiah, who was known to have a tender heart and for being sensitive towards the Lord's heart, carried many words about the shepherds of Israel. In an early prophecy, he declares that the Lord will give Israel "shepherds after His own heart" (Jeremiah 3:15) and later rebukes shepherds who divide, destroy, neglect or scatter His flock (Jeremiah 23). Towards the middle of Jeremiah's prophetic career, God speaks to him what Jesus would echo in His earthly ministry, that He would gather Israel like a shepherd. And there is a very revealing moment where Jeremiah shows how God intends to restore Israel, by putting shepherds in the wildernesses and cities (Jeremiah 33:12). It is always God's intention to pastor His flock through leaders who will take care of His people's hearts.

A refreshed definition is particularly important for this chapter because of the ubiquity of the title "pastor" in the Western church culture. But it is also important to examine what makes a Pastor tick. What are the inner-workings of the mind and heart of this personality Tribe? We have done the broad strokes; let's add some texture to the canvas to really see the portrait of the Pastor.

Pastoral Mindsets and Attitudes

If you talk to a Pastor, one of the major words that resonate inside of them is "Family." They consider the way that everything affects everyone. It is about the individual, but it is also about how the individual connects to the whole. Pastors want connection and security to mark their community. Accomplishment comes second to unity. The entire community may be efficiently running and advancing, but it doesn't matter if individuals are offended, neglected, or forgotten. Jesus' parable about the shepherd who leaves the flock of 99 to find the 1 is a perfect example of this; 99% is not a passing score for Pastor, because every heart is important. It isn't "one team, one dream" with a Pastor; it is "no one left behind."

Not only is a Pastor's mind always set on the family, but they are equally oriented towards unifying the corporate heart. Just as the Evangelist cares for the Will of the community, a Pastor cares for the Heart of the community. When the Apostle has a vision for the community, the high priority of the Pastor is that each individual is in heart agreement with the vision. They are not so concerned with them understanding the apostolic vision practically, unless that will help them embrace it fully in their heart. The Pastor wants the people to feel comfortable with and trust what is going on around them. So when the Prophet of the community comes to redirect something, the Pastor quickly scans the flock for offense and takes on the mission of reuniting the heart of the flock to the prophetic direction of the community. They will take whatever amount of time necessary to hear people out and restore relationship or heart-agreement with where the group is going.

Don't get the wrong impression; Pastors are not just damage control for the emotionally wounded. They will inevitably do a lot of damage control and relational restoration, but they are much more than that. Pastors go beyond helping people agree with the culture of the community, Pastors live to see people inspired. There is nothing quite as fulfilling to a Pastor than when they can inspire passion in someone to live life fully, openly, and freely. When someone is down or depressed or disconnected, Pastors don't just want to get them back to ground zero; they want to light a fire under them and desire to instill ecstatic happiness, excitement, and interconnectedness.

True Pastors want their flock so connected and fulfilled by their community family that the sheep become shepherds. The protected become protectors. As with all of the Five, the purpose of the Pastor in a community is to empower others to be Shepherd Snipers with them. This is not so that they don't have to do as much work, but so that the community as a whole is safer and more fulfilling and able to flourish. They want to preserve the happy fulfillment of hearts connected to the head. Far from being on mutiny patrol, Pastors lay down their lives and comfort for the chance for their community to have a thriving, vibrant culture (John 10:11).

Strengths and Struggles

It isn't hard to see how important a Pastor is to the success of a community. They are lovingly peaceful and kindly patient. You can recognize a Pastor by simply thinking of people who you feel safe around. They are the type of people that carry an atmosphere around them that makes you feel like everything will be all right, no matter what happens you know that they will take care of anything that will be disruptive or dangerous. In conversations with Pastors, you feel cared for. You could share anything with them and they will really hear you, truly see you, and will not evaluate you based on your issues, but rather will walk with you through whatever emotional swamp you find yourself in. Pastors easily give you the benefit of the doubt and want to help you find peace in the storm or a solution to lighten the burden on your shoulders.

The absence of a Pastor in a community becomes extremely evident after you have experienced the presence of one. They make the difference between a "community" and a "company," between an "organic fellowship" and an "organizational partnership," or between a "home" and a "residence." They carry the intangibles of successful community development. In the presence of a Pastor, you aren't "doing research," you are "discovering." Everything seems more alive and robust when you are in a community where you feel like you are with "your people." This is the contribution of the Pastor, everyone feels like they belong and are appreciated and important to the Family.

It is important for the sake of having a successful and happy community to value people for what they bring to the table. The tendency of most people is to hear the squeaky wheel on the cart rather than appreciate the heavy load the cart is making easier to move. At the same time, ignoring limitations is foolishness.

With Pastors, one of the main limitations is they can be impractically people-oriented. When an Apostle has set the culture and is trying to push forward with the Prophet in advancing that culture, a Pastor can have the tendency to slow things down immensely by drawing the attention to the people's needs. A Teacher will think that the Pastor is "gumming up the cogs" with all their cries of "what about the *people*?!" And though that will sound insensitive to you Pastors who are reading this, there is some real truth to it. And it is sometimes wisdom to just let people's hearts catch up on the road to advancement. Coddling people can lead to codependence and stagnation.

But in the end, people are important. And most of what Jesus taught had to do with how to interact with people – how to love and care for people.

Examples – Biblical, Historical, and Fictional

Jesus is the Shepherd of all shepherds, and is *always* the quintessential example for us in giving us a life to emulate in all things. With the Pastor, it is no different, but here are some more scriptural nuggets for you to chew on. Jesus calls Himself "the Good Shepherd" in John 10, and echoes the Old Testament prophet's picture of a Shepherd being struck down and the sheep scattering in Mark 14 and Matthew 26. He also shows His Shepherd's heart in Matthew 9 and Mark 6, seeing the disoriented crowds as sheep without a Shepherd. Isn't it also interesting that the angelic announcement of His birth went to a group of shepherds?

In Numbers 11 we see an interesting scene where the Lord imparts the mantle of Moses to the elders of the people. And even though two of them don't come to the meeting, they still get the impartation and begin to prophesy in the camp. Joshua comes to Moses, concerned for the implications and affects that Eldad and Medad's prophesying would have on the people and on Moses. In a way, Joshua was voicing a Pastoral concern – though Moses rebukes him for not having the big picture.

During his war-stricken day, Winston Churchill was a Pastor to both his nation and the world. Not only did he lead and have prophetic foresight into what would result from the social and political climate, but also in his radio addresses he pastorally appealed to the hearts of his hearers. He wanted people to connect in their heart with the global crises. For him it was not about a national opinion or political perspective, it was about sheep in search of truth to free their hearts. From his place of influence he was perfectly positioned to be a Sniper Shepherd.

One of the best moments in the parable of Ecclon that exemplifies Patrick as the Pastor is when Piper comes with the warning. Patrick's first reaction is concern for how the people will take the news. He immediately empathizes with Piper's rejection and offers to go with her to help, knowing that his personality would lubricate the relational friction. Patrick's Pastor status is also evident by how family oriented he is. He loves his own family, he appeals to Fort Follis as a family man, and when the other villages send their people to New Ecclon, what is his reaction? Throw a party to celebrate them and welcome them into the family.

As we wrap up the explanation chapters next with the Teacher, keep in mind that just understanding your personality Tribe is only the first step in having quality connections. Understanding the other Four and grasping how to interact with them is just as critical in having a community with a pulse. In the chapters to come the whole picture will become more lucid and applicable.

Teachers:
a Tribe of Designers and Explainers

The Parable of Ecclon: Thatcher

Thatcher was involved in every single step of the process that Andrew did while colonizing the valley. Thatcher had a way of being prepared with plans and contingency plans before Andrew ever asked for them. With the new additions to New Ecclon (the families from Fort Follis and Benton) there was inevitably going to be a lot of construction and other village developmental planning. Thatcher would be Andrew's greatest asset in accomplishing all that would be done in the valley.

The leaders of the three villages gathered in New Ecclon to go over Thatcher's plans. After exchanging pleasantries, Andrew turned to Thatcher and asked, "How much would it take to prevent New Ecclon from an avalanche or a washout flood? We want to take care of that first so that we can send our people to help the other villages."

Thatcher looked up from the paper he was scratching out plans on while they had been talking. "Well, we are mostly protected here on the low plateau at the base of the mountain. We chose this spot strategically to avoid mountain run-off." Andrew interjected, "Don't you mean, YOU chose this spot strategically?" Andrew bit his lip to keep from smiling at his trusted friend, Thatcher.

Unaffected by the playful honor, and very focused on the tasks at hand, Thatcher continued. "Benton will be most devastated by a washout because it is on the riverbank, while Fort Follis will be crushed if the avalanche comes first. According to my calculations, New Ecclon will only need minor preparations to avoid damage of any sort."

Thatcher's schedule was right on. A small avalanche was redirected away from Fort Follis. A week later, the displaced snow melted, but the floodwaters only touched the homes closest to the river in Benton. At Thatcher's suggestion, Benton housing had been moved north and just the docks and fish processing buildings remained near the river. In the process of building the avalanche wall, some of the New Ecclonians had moved closer to Fort Follis, giving their old homes to the Bentonians who moved away from the river. The result was a connecting of the hearts and the borders of the three towns.

Thus the valley city of Haven was founded.

A Re-definition of "Teacher"

Have you ever noticed in movies there are cliché characters? In dramas and action flicks there is the token genius. This is the guy who is always a bit disheveled, wears clothes that are about half a decade out of style, and who seems to always nervously reveal critical information slightly out of time. There's a problem with writing a book about personality Tribes in a media-obsessed culture. When I say "Teacher," automatically we think of either an eccentric brainiac or a boring Oxford professor with chalk dust on the leather elbow patches on his wool sports coat.

This is not what a Teacher is, at least not in the fullest sense.

The Teacher of Ephesians 4 is the word *'didaskalos'*, it is used almost five dozen times in the New Testament. The verb that this title comes from is a prolonged form of a base verb meaning "to learn." In other words, a Teacher could be said to be one who has given their lives to learning – both their own learning and the learning of those around them.

They are Master Learners.

They have learned how to learn. And they possess true understanding. The Hebrew concept of "understanding" carries a sense of being able to break something down into its parts – separating or disassembling an idea as a demonstration of discernment. If you have ever been around Jewish men discussing a matter, you have seen how ideas are picked apart with carefully crafted questions. They will dissect and examine every component of an idea. This is what impressed the Rabbis about the boy Jesus, He asked poignant questions (Luke 2:47). And He continued in the rabbinic style of teaching during His earthly ministry. And in my experience with Him lately, He is still a fan of asking questions to provoke me to think and understand.

On the other side of the coin, the Greek concept of "understanding" carries a sense of being able to bring two things together – assembling or assimilating ideas as a demonstration of mastery. This is why Paul had to write his letter to Colossae, they had become proficient in the Greek culture at mixing religions. This is called "syncretism," and it is an issue today as well. It was so prevalent in those days that one of the forms of entertainment was that philosophically minded men would sit around and just share new ideas they had mixed up. But Paul fought hard to keep the Gospel pure and unmixed with the culture of the day.

The passion of a Teacher is to fully understand whatever is set before them. Whether it is theological minutiae, how people from up north can stand the cold easier than southerners (I still don't get that one), or why three more coffee beans changes the flavor of an espresso shot so much; Teachers are haunted by the question, "Why?" If there ends up being an application for their understanding, that is a bonus. But the understanding, and the journey to understanding, is what really fulfills a Teacher.

One of Jesus' most common titles in the gospels is "Rabbi." Most of these references are in the context of him explaining a hard truth, a parable or some other mystery of the Kingdom. But even when they are not in that context, Jesus had a reputation for excellent answers to difficult questions (John 16:30) – even among the brilliant Scribes. But one can only appear so brilliant when the Light of the World is next to you. Jesus masterfully silenced the false wisdom of the Scribes and Pharisees.

One night, in a secret meeting, Jesus spoke with a Jewish leader and rebuked him for being known as "the teacher of Israel," but not being able to understand simple things of the Kingdom (John 3). Apparently Jesus expected a Teacher to be able to grasp a concept, even if it were new to them. Paul takes it a step further in a letter correcting an Italian church split, saying that teachers ought to prove their understanding by applying it to their own lives (Romans 2). And he could hold them to the high standard that James wrote about, because God had appointed him as "a teacher of the Gentiles" (1 Timothy 2:7 and 2 Timothy 1:11).

With such easy access to information, we do not have a high value on teachers unless they can wrap up their How-To video on YouTube in under 4 minutes. But in the first century, it was a different story.

Paul warned Timothy that the false believers that were plotting against his congregation would acquire teachers that taught what would not conflict with their desires (2 Timothy 4:3). He understood that a Teacher does not just explain concepts; they set up systems of belief and behavior in a community. To the Corinthian church, Paul explained that Apostles come first, then Prophets second and the third essential element in developing a church was the Teachers (1 Corinthians 12:28). This is because Teachers create the structures and systems that act as the framing for a community's culture. Jesus even said that Teachers that practice their own teaching are called great in the Kingdom (Matthew 5:19).

Teachers are not just information collectors. They are dynamically minded; they like the details and think of the implications or effects of the little things. You want a Teacher to be your surgeon, your mechanic, and your CPA. But they aren't just detailed administrative people; they have a passion to make things run smoothly, maximize efficiency and remove the extra parts. They design structures that bring freedom and create systems that ensure flexibility for people to be unique and expressive. When instructing Timothy about the Ephesian church plant leadership, Paul told him to teach Paul's teachings to reliable men so that they could also teach them to the people (2 Timothy 2:2). Paul was helping Timothy design a sustainable system of instruction in Ephesus. He maintains this sentiment in writing to Thessalonica, telling them to "hold fast to the traditions and instructions which you were taught" (2 Thessalonians 2:15).

In considering the Teacher, remember that the movie nerd is not what we are talking about. The Teacher is not a walking brain; Teachers are passionate and even emotional. Almost no one is purely one personality Tribe, as if developed in a sterile laboratory where robot-Teachers are uploaded with a program. We will go more in depth soon about being more than one of the Five, but for now let's look at the nuances of the Teacher's inner workings.

Teacher Mindsets and Attitudes

The key word I want you to associate with the mindset of a Teacher is "dynamic." Teachers, when fully empowered and endorsed, are free to evaluate and process details without feeling restricted. A Teacher loves to be creative in discovering solutions to problems or designing preventative solutions to potential problems. Call them a nerd if you want, but that nerd just may be the very one making your life much easier in the near future.

The orientation of the Teacher is usually very practical and about full understanding. They want their community to think right. We saw that the Evangelist was the inspirer of the community's Will. And the Pastor's obsession is the community's Heart – both individual and corporate. The Teacher is the guardian of the Mind. On an oversight level, the Teacher will design systems and structures to ensure community quality control, but on a face-to-face level, a Teacher wants nothing more than for the person in front of them to have an "Ah-hah" moment. When something clicks in someone's mind, the Teacher feels life flood his or her being.

As Designers, they look not only at function but the psychological impact on the community. Their joy is not in their own experience but in the satisfactory experience of others. Teachers are the party planners who are just as into the decorations as they are into the invitations, the food selection for vegetarians, and the plan for the clean up at the end of the night.

As Explainers, their fulfillment comes from others really encountering the joy that they have in understanding something. Think of the wacky science teacher you had in high school who geeked out over chemical reactions, physics experiments, or biology facts. When you're a student, you kind of look at them as an alien species. But think back to the moments when you were working on a project or homework. There must have been a moment for you like there was for me, when I suddenly didn't just know how to regurgitate information, but I actually *got it!* It wasn't just completing my homework anymore; it was grasping the universal laws of calculus and physics. These are the moments that Teachers live to experience and to give to others.

I have been discipling people for years now. The Teacher in me takes so much joy in those moments where Truth breaks in, freeing my disciples' minds and hearts simultaneously. It is not just the truth that sets us free, but it is the truth that we know that sets us free (John 8:32). And that, my friends, is a Teacher's heartbeat.

Strengths and Struggles

It is easy to get into stereotyping when identifying personality Tribes. But there is some helpful truth to be found in creating categories to distinguish tendencies. For example, you may be a Teacher but what I am about to say about the Teacher Tribe may not apply to you. Or maybe it will only partially apply to you. In any case, continue to look at these as base colors, from which you will find a specific hue that you most identify with or with which you feel most comfortable.

Due to the nature of the Teacher as an Explainer, there is a strong value on organization. It is hard to explain something that you haven't organized your thoughts about. But organization does not necessarily mean neat. Creative people are organized, not like auditors have to be, but in a vibrant way. In any case, the prototypical Teacher is creatively and vibrantly organized. This can look like filing systems or flow charts or piles that require the pile-maker to decipher, but in whatever way a Teacher organizes, there is intentionality and their personality infused in structures they employ.

My dad is an incredibly creative person. His mind is like a filing cabinet with Rubik's Cube locks. He graduated high school third in his class only because he got one B in a Chemistry class.

Then in college he was an Education Major with a double Minor in Social Science and Russian. Though he has always been an incredibly creative person, it costs money to raise children. So he went back to school to get his MBA in Accounting. During his entire life in education, his GPA average was just short of 3.8 for all three degrees he earned. Obviously his organizational brain works, but hibernating inside was always a wild, creative genius. After becoming an auditor for the state of Michigan and similar subsequent jobs, eventually he retired. Ever since then his life has been a creative explosion. On our semi-regular Skype calls with my parents, one of the subjects that will typically come up is what new project he is working on.

This rubbed off on my younger brother and me as well. We both got perfect scores on the national Advanced Placement Calculus exams. But we both also became musical and led worship at various ministries. I even recorded a four-track demo at a co-worker's home studio, all songs that I wrote. This demo will never be released – do not ask. I was an artist and my first job was as a graphic artist at age 16, while my brother was in choir and theatre. We were both heavily involved in church activities and school athletics. The difference? He went into the medical field and I went into ministry. But we both picked up that creative yet organized style from our dad.

What am I saying? Teachers are brilliant and they love to use their brilliant minds to influence what is around them. Secondly, Teachers are reliable and willing to work hard on hard projects or activities. This comes from the tendency to pay close attention to details and to value things being done correctly. It doesn't bother a Teacher that they lost out on social interactions while working on something, designing something, or discovering something new. If you are leading a Teacher, and you recognize it in them, you can trust that if they have a task put before them, it will be done right. They may take more time on it than you deem necessary, but the integrity or quality of the completed task need not be in questions.

This will likely not come as a surprise to anyone, but there is a down side to the grand focus of a Teacher. Though helpful for someone who doesn't want to do the work, for the one trying to get something done quickly or who is seeing the bigger picture, it is not such a positive aspect of the Teacher's personality. They can be rigid and immovably myopic. Particularly if the Teacher gets really focused on the importance of what they are working on, there is a potential for friction to encroach on the relational side.

We have seen with each of the Five there are potential limitations to overcome. These do not have to be deal-breaking relationship destroyers. It is wise to keep these things in mind as indicators of a personality Tribe and as something to be prepared for in case it does manifest. But we will deal with how to interact with each of the Five in later chapters.

Examples – Biblical, Historical, and Fictional

Already we have sufficiently seen how Jesus was a Teacher. So I will rescue you from an unnecessarily pedantic exposition of our Rabbi's "Teacher-ness." However, Jesus does make a few interesting statements about the other Two in the Godhead concerning Their "Teacher-ness". Of the Holy Spirit, He said in Luke 12 that the Spirit would teach – not *tell* – the disciples what to say when put on the spot in times of persecution. Then in John 14, Jesus says that the Spirit will teach the disciples *all things*. That is a pretty hefty promise that I intend to take Him up on in the age to come. As for the Father, we are familiar with Jesus' statement that He only did what He saw the Father doing (John 5:19). But less famous is His statement in John 8, where Jesus reveals that He only said the things that the Father had *taught* Him. The implications of this are staggering, especially in light of the understanding of Jesus as our ultimate example of belief and behavior.

Another great Biblical example of a Teacher in Scripture is Paul. Not only did he explain Kingdom principles masterfully, but also in his teachings and letters, he crafted systems of thinking and structures of belief that would sustain the communities he was apostolically discipling. Any serious student of the New Testament will likely confess their deep appreciation for the way that Paul constructs his letters. He was a literary ninja, leading his readers to conclusions through provoking questions in their hearts – and then answering the very questions he was leading them to ask. That is a skill that only a Teacher can wield.

However, as we have been looking at the Teacher, we have seen how being a Teacher is not about teaching information necessarily. The essence of a Teacher is dynamic systems and creative structures that guide a community to its end goal. No one exemplifies this better in the Scriptures than Joseph. In partnership with God, Joseph saved Egypt by setting up an economic system to prepare for a coming famine. Not only did Joseph act as a Prophet to declare what was coming, he acted as a Teacher in crafting a creative way to avoid the potential destruction of the immanent famine.

Speaking of economics, Dave Ramsey is a wonderful picture of a Teacher. This is not because he has teaching series and radio shows and conferences and books. He is a Teacher because he has created systems of thinking that have transformed the financial culture of many Christian and non-Christian families. He is experienced and truly understands the ins and outs of debt, financial freedom, and economics in general. His wisdom and structured explanations are extremely helpful. They have helped me get out of credit card debt and were instrumental in helping me to understand financial principles that freed me up in my 20s to pay no rent for years.

Thatcher is the Teacher of the Parable of Ecclon. Thatcher was always coming up with solutions and plans and ideas, even before the discussion had come to asking the questions that he was answering. Andrew and the other leaders came to depend on and expect Thatcher to be who he was, and did not try to do his job.

We will discuss the church-specific application of the Five in “Five in the Box”. Then we will look at how the Five can be applied in the real world, since only a small minority is called to church service occupationally. This is where the theorizing becomes a little more practical and applicable. It will get more so as we continue on. So hang in there, there are further depths to the rabbit hole.

But before we do that, let's attempt to answer the question that almost everyone asks at this point in teaching on the Five: can I be more than one of the Five?

Five-Fold Schizophrenia: Can I Be More Than One?

Be You, However That Looks: Empowered Uniqueness

Whether you are a current leader, a future leader, a lone ranger, or an enthusiastic follower, identity is key to your success. Leaders must empower and celebrate the uniqueness of those they lead. Not only do people hate being put in categorical boxes, but also it is ineffective leadership and will lead to more problems in the end. It takes time and effort to know the people that you labor through life with. However, the reward far out-weighs the investment.

As followers, we will be less frustrated, more productive, and happier when we can see our leaders for who they are. That kind of clarity empowers us to follow well. But as the old mystic once said, "seek to understand more than to be understood." We will be held accountable for our actions, thoughts, and words, not those of the people who lead us.

You may be a lone ranger, an independent free spirit, or just a normal leader or follower, we all must know and love our selves first. Then, we can know and love our neighbor in the same way. The real you is going to look different from how anyone else looks, and probably different from how you currently look. But the most liberating feeling you will ever experience is when you know that you can live unbridled and remain fully endorsed. You can be you, fully and unreservedly. No matter what that looks like, it is your responsibility to display to the world the glories hidden only in you.

The raw truth is this: if you do not manifest the fullness of who you are to the world around you, the world will not be able to come into its fullness. We rob the world of our flavor contribution by being an anemic version of ourselves. God likes how He made you and if other people cannot agree with His opinion of you, then they miss out on the unique embrace that He can give them uniquely through you. This is why Jesus told His disciples to go into cities and love on people like He demonstrated, but if they didn't listen to or receive the disciples, then they were released to go somewhere where they would embrace Him as expressed through them (Matthew 10:14). You see, people aren't rejecting you, they are rejecting Him because of the package He has wrapped Himself in – you. This is normal Christian life; Jesus was rejected because of His packaging. In fact, one of the reasons Satan fell was that he got offended at the humanity of Christ (see Jeremiah 14 and Ezekiel 28).

As you lead, follow and live, always empower people's uniqueness. When people trip up over your uniqueness, help them, but do not change who you are. Abraham Lincoln said, "We can complain because rose bushes have thorns, or rejoice because thorn bushes have roses." As image-bearers, people deserve the freedom that comes from being celebrated, endorsed, and believed in no matter how that manifests.

Unfortunately, we cannot truly and fully know our own value. Short of being pulled out of reality and shown what things would be like without your contribution to society, like in the classic Christmas movie *It's a Wonderful Life*, we have to be told our value from an external source. And then we have to believe it. You simply have never been in a room that you were not in or in a conversation that you were not present for. So you cannot know what it is like when you are not around. You carry something that changes the very atmosphere of a room, a situation, a conversation, or an interaction. It is not necessarily what you do, but who you are that changes the nature of every place you choose to breath the air. God told Joshua that everywhere he put his foot would be transformed into the Kingdom he represented (Joshua 1:3). It is the same for you.

Nuances: Overview of The Shades of Your Personality

The most common question I hear other than "Which of the Five do you think I am?" is "Can I be more than one of the Five?" The short answer is "yes...kind of."

As I have looked at the Five as personality Tribes, it became imperative to answer this question because the lines are blurry from person to person. Almost no one is purely one or another. There are shades of each in just about everyone.

At the very core of who you are, there is one primary tendency that you manifest all the time. You manifest in one way or another, no matter what situation you are in or who you are with. This is what we will call your "Main Tribe." You will find that you identify most strongly with one and people who think like that one. Those people are part of your Tribe; though we are all part of one race, or Kingdom, we have a certain kind of person that we feel closer to. Our Main Tribe is who thinks like us the most and understands us best because they have similar experiences and perspectives towards life. The Main Tribe describes *who* you are, but is best discovered by answering the question "why?" in regular life.

If you have ever taken a personality test, they normally have you note your second highest score. It helps to know what else you are leaning towards. Your secondary of the Five, normally different from your primary, we will call your "Manner." This is the adjectival application of the Five. For example, you may be a *pastoral* prophet, meaning that you are in the Prophet Tribe, but amidst your Prophet-like tendencies, you lean towards the heart of a Pastor in the *way* that you do things. We will describe this in better detail in the following sections. But the Manner describes *how* you do what you do.

The first two nuances are a little more ethereal than the third, which we will call your "Method." Your Method is your skill-set and the tools that you use to accomplish the goals that are set before you. You may be a pastoral Prophet with a Teacher gift. This would be someone who is Main Tribe Prophet (shifter and sculptor of culture), but they carry themselves within that Tribe like a Pastor, and they use the Teacher gift to accomplish things.

They would teach, train, equip, and explain a lot, so people may think they are a Teacher. But the reason they teach, train, equip, and explain is to sculpt and shape culture in a heart-oriented manner. The Method describes *what* you do.

There may even be a fourth nuance to this whole thing, which we will call your "Mark." In my observations, very few people have a Mark that is completely different from the other three nuances. But it is possible, for the more complex people. The Mark is the contribution that someone has on a community. You could say this is someone's "calling" (but that would not fit the alliteration of M's, and alliteration is essential to effective teaching). So, someone may be a pastoral Prophet with a Teacher gift and an Apostolic Mark (or calling). This would be just like the person we have described, but the ultimate result of their sculpting the hearts of the community through teaching is that they establish culture. The Mark describes what you *contribute* to your community.

The following sections will flesh out these concepts a little more. This is not exhaustive, nor is it a perfect model. But it can be helpful in the pursuit of understanding yourself and others. The nuances are the shades of the painting of who you are, but they are not even the deep details of your identity. Someone could be identical to you in his or her Main Tribe, Manner, Method, and Mark, but they will inevitably manifest those things differently from you. Every snowflake, though composed of the same material, looks different.

Why You Do: Explanation of Your "Main Tribe"

One aspect of natural tribes is that people think similarly because they have their worldview shaped by their surroundings, teaching, and influences. With the Five, you will find that you think like one particular Main Tribe more than the others. This has less to do with who has externally taught you, and more to do with how you have been crafted by God.

One of the best ways I have found to discover someone's Main Tribe is to ask them why they do something. Then, when they answer that, I again ask "but, Why?" And somewhere down the Why Road it becomes clear what their "Ultimate Why" is, and by that it is easy to identify which Main Tribe they identify with most strongly. The important thing, for you or for someone you are instructing, is for the answers to be honest and candid.

Often people will answer questions a certain way based on the teaching they have received, the positions they have been in, the experiences that they have had, or the people that are hearing their answers. If you really want to get to the bottom of this thing, you are going to have to be brutally honest and deal with the consequences after you have settled on the truth. I had an intern once who had bad experiences with pastors, so whenever someone told him he was pastoral, he would strongly react. His experiences had shaped his opinion of what it is to be a Pastor. Since having a more positive experience with a true Pastor, his value for the pastoral position has changed.

How You Do: Explanation of Your "Manner"

Let's say there was a gathering of Teachers. Within this group, because they would all have a primary similarity, each would begin to manifest their secondary, or "Manner." One would consider it essential to teach and train as a way to strengthen culture – an Apostolic Manner. Another would begin to teach outsiders about their great culture – an Evangelistic Manner. The third would want people to understand in their hearts, because he is a "Pastoral Teacher". The fourth would be solely concerned about the corporate belief structure – a pure Teacher. And a fifth may want to teach so as to change something in the culture – a Prophetic Teacher.

It is easiest to see the secondary Manner when the primary Main Tribe is removed. This happens mostly in situations where your primary strength is covered by an oversaturation of "fellow tribesmen." My mother always taught me to be a man able to fill gaps, so I learned multiple instruments so I could play on worship teams no matter who couldn't make it. Though my strongest instrument was guitar, if a bassist, pianist, or even a drummer was needed, I was ready. In the same way, what you most easily convert over to when your primary strength is not needed is your secondary Manner.

It is also the way you manifest your strength. Do you create culture that is heart-focused? You may be a Pastoral Apostle. Do you affect change to draw people to something or some place that impacted you? You may be a Prophetic Evangelist. Do you find yourself consistently explaining how things work and helping others understand how things are supposed to be? You may be an Apostolic Teacher.

Or maybe you don't have a secondary Manner, you're just a pure Pastor. That's a good thing too. It doesn't stop at why or how you do something. What you do is another factor all together. This is where it gets even more practical.

What You Do: Explanation of Your "Method"

If you have ever tried to get to know someone with no prior knowledge of them, you are familiar with that typical first question: "So, what do you do?" If you have ever been on the receiving end of that question, you know full well that they are asking the wrong question. What you do is not who you are, so why is that our first question when trying to get to know someone else?

The Method is where most people get hung up and misunderstood, by being categorized wrongly and not valued for who they truly are. But once you have gotten past these hang-ups, and can recognize the *why* and the *how* of each person's identity, then you can truly appreciate the Method that each person employs. These are the gifts that you use. And gifts can be cultivated or ignored, depending on the value that the receiver puts on each gift. Gifts can also be circumstantial. Like we saw in the prior section on "Manner," sometimes a gift is not needed.

When I started working for MorningStar University, the position that was open was more of an administrative position. I was faithful to do what was necessary to keep my position, but when more and more opportunities came to teach and pastor students, my primary function changed. In fact, at a staff meeting one time, Rick Joyner said to me, "We need to hire you an assistant and get you off of the administration so that you can focus on pastoring the students." Thereafter, my primary function was to be the Student Pastor. However, I am neither a Pastor nor a Teacher in my Main Tribe. But I did function as both as the need arose. I used those pastoral and teaching gifts to maintain the culture of MorningStar University that Rick Joyner and my predecessors had created.

What You Contribute: Explanation of your "Mark"

The apostle Paul wrote to the church of Rome explaining that the gifts and callings of God remain with someone regardless of their depth of relationship with Him (Romans 11:29). As you may have noticed by now, this is true of the four nuances of the perspective we are taking on the Five in this book. Whether someone is a "hardcore Christian," a backslider, or a pagan, you can see built into everyone around you some measure of these characteristics. It is their "calling" - what God has called, or named, them. Your Mark on the situations around you is going to be fairly consistent, no matter how close to God you think you are.

Everyone has a specific impact on the interactions they have. Whether those interactions are long-term relationships, momentary acquaintances, or just a single meeting, we always leave some sort of lasting impression. That can be an indication of what your Mark is, mostly in the long-term relationships, but also in shorter interactions. Think about people you know. One person may affect you in how you understand life; they give you perspective and thought-structure to life. Their Mark is probably as a Teacher. Or maybe you have a friend that is always creating change in your life, helping you see new things that are available, and helping you avoid roadblocks in your way towards success. Their Mark is as a Prophet. Someone with a Pastor's Mark will leave you feeling loved, cared for, and empowered to be fully you. One with an Evangelist's Mark would be that friend or family member who is always telling you about exciting new books, movies, and other experiences that they think you would benefit from. Whereas an Apostle's Mark comes with someone who inspires you to assimilate into the culture that they carry, not in a needy or manipulative way, but true inspiration.

Many times a person's Mark is the same is their Main Tribe. However, I have encountered people who seemed to have a slightly different Mark from their other nuances. One friend, in particular, is a Pure Teacher with Pastor's Method, but what results in every situation I have seen him in is strongly Apostle-like. And ultimately, as Christians, we are all called to have the effect on society around us that causes us to establish the culture of the Kingdom. So in some sense, all Christians should have a hint of Apostle in their Mark. But it is unwise to limit the expression possibilities when God has made us all completely different.

Five In the Box:
a How-To Guide to Congregational Functions

Prerequisite Proviso

Before we discuss the way that each of the Five optimally function in a church setting, I want to be clear on how to understand and apply this chapter. Most importantly, our mentality towards the Five must come from Ephesians 4, which says that each of the Five are given as a gift to the body, and that the purpose of the Five is to train others to walk in the fullness of what they carry. Being a leader in a church, or any leadership position for that matter, means that the person leading is giving their life to lifting others up and advancing them. It is not for self-fulfillment or personal advancement. Leading is about the follower, not the leader.

However, each of the Five can manifest in people without an official or recognized position. There are specific ways that these personality Tribes are expressed within churches uniquely from in the world. As an Evangelist is discipled by the church's leading Evangelist, they will progressively become more genuinely themselves and this will result in a powerful demonstration of their true identity.

There are official and semi-official positions in churches in the 21st century that did not exist in the 1st century, or that looked quite different twenty centuries ago. For example, in the early Church there were multiple bishops to one church, but now we have bishops over multiple churches. Then there are positions like "Worship Leader," "Intercessor," and other functions that are helpful and normal in our day that were not as present in the infancy of the Church. Other positions have remained but have taken on new forms in some streams but stayed the same in others. For example, in some denominations a "deacon" is more than it used to be, in others the position has consistently been recognition of service and responsibility, and in still others most congregation members would believe you if you told them that "deacons" are the personal bodyguards for the Pope.

Disclaimer for those not employed by their church: the purpose of this chapter and this book is not to give you ammo to shoot at how your church is doing it wrong. If you do not have the authority in your church to change something or the means to introduce new ideas, do not judge your church or its leaders. Judgment will only negatively affect your access to authority. Rather, simply begin to recognize and identify how things work at your church. Then you can easily adapt your perspective to function within your church at present. If, in the future, you find yourself in a greater position of authority, you will have discerned the body rightly and will thus be better prepared to make suggestions and assist in a transition to a new mentality in your church.

Maybe you are reading this and you are starting a church, ministry or organization. If that is the case, do not wait to have a person in place for each of the Five before you step out to do what the Lord has shown you to do. These positions should fill themselves organically. Appointing someone to a position just to fill the position can be detrimental to their growth and your success. We will discuss being misplaced in a later chapter. All that to say, be faithful to step into your assignment and keep your eyes peeled to see whom the Lord brings to you. The reality is that this structure takes time to develop and perfect. If you are starting off, you can lay a good foundation in preparation but it will grow with your church naturally. If you are trying to change the organization chart to establish these roles, it will take time to get everyone to understand and get on board with the changes. Have patience. Also, know that more important than an altered organization chart is the recognition of how people are ALREADY functioning and then empowering them in their unique contribution.

Each of the Five are needed. Not only to lead, but, until all of the members of the Body know who they are and are walking in the fullness of Christ. The Five are needed to mature the body in a healthy and vibrant culture. The purpose of the positions in a church is to have leaders who can train and equip people that are like themselves. It is of paramount importance to understand that the job of a leader is to make room for their replacement. As we move towards the Church being a family and not a non-profit organization, we will see the wisdom of turning our attention to the future and laying the right foundation for where we are going.

Apostles

Whether someone has "Apostle" on their business card or not is irrelevant. Every church has someone functioning as an Apostle to that church. They are the leader, the authoritative human hub who carries, creates, and maintains the culture of that church. In order to fully catch the wave of what is going on at a church, the key is to be aligned with the Apostle. Not only is it our job to recognize who carries the apostolic authority in our churches, it is vital that we follow well and honor their decisions. In the eyes of the Lord, the responsibility for the church is on the Apostolic leader. So when they make decisions, whether we agree with the decision or not, our job is to get behind them and lean into the vision of the church.

Sometimes the vision of a church comes by a commissioning from the Lord, sometimes it is inherited from the mother church that a church-plant is birthed from. In either case, the carrier of that vision and the responsibility for the implementation of that vision is on the Apostle. Paul wrote that the mystery of Christ had been concealed for generations but had been revealed to the Apostles and Prophets (Colossians 1:27). And though he was referring to the Apostles and Prophets of the Bible, it applies to us now in that God gives spiritual blueprints to those leading His churches. When Paul wrote to Corinth, he said that Apostles always come first, then Prophets and Teachers (1 Corinthians 12:28). We must humbly accept the fact that we don't know everything that God is doing, support our leaders and trust Him to guide and lead them.

The Apostle of a church will not just make decisions and lead, they are also designed to disciple and train other Apostles to do what they do. Moses' father-in-law rebuked Moses for trying to lead Israel alone (Exodus 18:18). If that was true of a man who had face-to-face intimacy with God, it is true of us. Jethro's advice to Moses was to impart what hc carried to others. This is the responsibility of the Five, to empower others to do what they do. At the outset of a church plant, the Apostle is the one who carries the responsibility to fulfill all the roles until a suitable leader is found or groomed to take that position. This is, perhaps, the reason that Paul told Timothy to do the work of an evangelist, because there had not yet been found someone to fill that slot. Until someone did, Timothy was in the apostolic position and it was his job to evangelize or train an evangelist.

By discipling and empowering other Apostles within their church, an Apostle can more effectively create culture and set the tone for the church. When I was Student Pastor at MorningStar University, I would spend time mostly with my interns, the influencers, and small group leaders. By doing this, I was able to keep from being overwhelmed with meetings, but still efficiently ensure that the culture of the school was maintained and flourishing.

This trickle-down principle is a pillar in my mentality of leadership. It is a strong motivator to pursue a dynamic inner life, as well as a deterrent from sin, knowing that what I carry will affect those I lead. I noticed this first when I was a student at MorningStar. Because of the prophetic anointing on my leaders, my prophetic ministry accuracy skyrocketed. But the principle became far more real to me when I was a leader and I noticed that small compromises in my heart translated into major problems that I had to deal with in the students I was leading. Both my strengths and my struggles trickled down.

The staggering truth is that we cannot just live our lives disconnected from the people around us. How I live my life in secret affects you, because we are all part of one Body. Apostles, in particular, are very influential members of the Body because they set the tone for everyone else. Those from a personality Tribe but not the position must recognize the influence they have and submit the power of their influence to the authority of their leaders or else they run the risk of participating in rebellion and leading a miniature reenactment of Korah's rebellion (Numbers 16).

Apostles are not always audible and outspoken leaders, though that is the tendency. There are people who create culture from behind the scenes. They serve and encourage and empower others in a way that unconsciously alters the culture that they operate in. These people are overlooked far too often, but are still an integral part of the creation and maintenance of church culture.

Prophets

In an official capacity, as we are looking at the Prophet as a Tribe, a church's Prophet is the second in command. Prophets are the Vice President, but it is very important to be a friend and partner with the Apostle. If the relational connection between leaders is strong, the church is strong. Church splits happen more often because of a breakdown in relationship, not so much for doctrinal reasons – though the easiest target to place blame on is doctrine or style. Particularly with the Prophet-Apostle relationship, friendship and camaraderie are vital. This is because one of the functions of the Prophet is to cover the blind spots of the Apostle. If there is weak connection between the top leaders, that will trickle down and fractures will become factions.

However, when relationship and responsibility are running smoothly and correctly, the Prophet serves as a confidant to the Apostle. The Prophet won't be critical of the Apostle, but will truly partner with the Apostle, look out for, defend, and even be sort of a pastor for the Apostle. But for the congregation, the Prophet is serving as a watchman. The Prophet devotes the majority of their time, energy, and resources to prevention of calamity and the capturing of opportunity. This comes by spending time with God, spending time walking with Him through the church (figuratively, but maybe physically as well) to continually steer the church towards the intended horizon.

In charismatic church circles, it will be hard to disconnect the *ministry* of a Prophet from the *function* of a Prophet. A church's Prophet is not necessarily the itinerate minister who comes through town periodically and gives inspiration and illumination to what the Lord is doing at that church, in that city, or globally. On the corporate level, a church's Prophet gives themselves to observing, listening, and staying connected to what is happening at the church. From this naturally and divinely informed crow's nest, they give correction to the church's direction.

The Prophets of the Bible, in both the Old and New Testaments, received their instructions from God directly and through the agency of angelic assistance. But rarely do we see a Prophet giving direction to a community, nation or church that they were not in some way invested in or connected to in real life. There are exceptions, like Jonah, but most of the Biblical Prophets had to live with the consequences of the reception of their words. Jeremiah was imprisoned (Jeremiah 37). The "two witnesses" of Revelation 11 are assassinated publicly.

The nature of the Prophets is primarily "bond-slaves" of the Lord. This is a term that Paul refers to himself as in his letters (Romans 1:1; 2 Corinthians 4:5; Galatians 1:10; Philippians 1:1; Titus 1:1), and John records the Twenty-Four Elders calling the Prophets (Revelation 1:1, 10:7 and 11:18). A "bond-slave" is not a random, extreme title used to illustrate the level of devotion within a person's heart to God. It is an intentional reference to a unique law in the Torah. Basically, if a man had become a slave to repay a debt, served the years necessary to repay the debt, but decided that he loved his master and wanted to continue serving him willfully, then he would become a "bond-slave." The formerly indebted slave chose not to be a free man but would go to the front door of his master's house and have an awl nailed through his ear lobe. He would wear this as a sign of his devotion all the days of his freewill service to his beloved master (Exodus 21).

That is what Paul and the Prophets carried in their hearts, a freewill, loving devotion to the Master. No compulsion or coercion, just radical devotion. And that is the nature of our Prophets today. They have a desire to prepare the Church for the coming of the Master who paid their debt and won their heart. John the Revelator called Moses a "bond-slave" in Revelation 15:3, and the prophet Moses called God "The God of the spirits of the prophets"

(Numbers 27:16). That is who He is to a Prophet; He is the God of their inner life and director of their outer life.

Peter eloquently explained the Prophets of old in his first letter. "The Prophets who prophesied of the grace that would come to you made careful searches and inquiries, seeking to know what person or time the Spirit of Christ within them was indicating...It was revealed to them that they were not serving themselves, but you" (1 Peter 1:10-13). The diligence of a Prophet to see what is coming is for the purpose of serving those to whom they speak, with the understanding that serving God's children is serving God by default.

So what does that look like in real church life? It could look different in each congregation. For the Corinthian church, Paul instructed them to allow prophets to stand up and give their messages in an orderly fashion (1 Corinthians 14:40). This was an encouragement to the historically chaotic church of Corinth to place the responsibility of orderly ministry times in the hands of the ministers. This is where Paul says, "the spirit of a prophet is subject to that prophet" in 1 Corinthians 14. In this section, Paul is calling this radically Spirit-filled church to hold its leaders to a high standard of conduct. He also says that those prophesying are to do so one at a time so that the words can be recorded and evaluated. A Prophet's words were never intended to be taken as infallible; they are people who only see part of what God sees (1 Corinthians 13:9).

It was the responsibility of Old Testament Prophets to appoint and anoint kings (1 Samuel 10:1). In the New Testament, a prophetic council in Acts 15 confirmed the authority on the lives of Judas and Silas and sent them to deliver a message to the churches in Antioch, Syria, and Cilicia. These and other places exemplify another responsibility of Prophets, to recognize authority on people and to commission people into service. This recognition is important because many times Jesus' words ring all too true that a Prophet is honored everywhere except at home. But Prophets, empathizing with this perceived rejection, are slated with the job of helping a church recognize each person for their unique anointing and contribution. The honoring of a person's calling is how the community can receive the reward that the Lord has deposited in their lives for those who would receive them rightly (Matthew 10:41f).

As with all of the Five, the Prophet of a church is not fulfilling their assignment fully until they have trained and equipped others to do what they do. Whether that means training up their replacement for when they leave their position or discipling those gifted similarly, they must empower others. If you think of a Prophet as a watchman, then it only makes sense that they create a team of Prophet-watchmen. If their church were a walled city, then the guarding of the walls could not be watched 24/7 by just one watchman. Eventually the one guard would fall asleep and leave the church unguarded. However, if the Prophet trains others, their job becomes oversight of the Prophet guardsmen on the wall of the church.

These other Prophet-guards are people with discernment of spirits, prophetic gifting, and foresight. Some prophets within a Church context will be worship leaders because they use their giftings and anointing to shift the atmosphere in a worship service. Or they will write songs that turn the hearts of the people toward God in a new way. Or maybe a Prophet will do a short teaching or exhortation to a small group or in a service, revealing some wonderful thing the Lord is showing them or doing in their life. There are really no limits to how a Prophet can express their personality. Artists and creative people are typically Prophets to some extent simply in the fact that they have the foresight of what has not been created, and they employ their gifts to create the future.

In a very real sense, every Christian has a little Prophet inside of them. We are shifters of atmospheres simply because we carry the Spirit, the Mighty Rushing Wind, within us. In the same way, we all have a little Apostle in us by the very nature of having been sent to this world for a certain purpose.

Evangelists

In college, I was a Bible Major with a double Minor in Philosophy and Ancient Languages. My favorite classes were

Biblical Greek and Biblical Criticism because of the intriguing little trinkets of revelation I got off of the teachings of Professors Smith and Brew. One such trinket was that in Greek the order of words is an indication of priority.

This does not just have to do with lists, but also the order of words within a normal sentence. It is a linguistic tool used to give emphasis, like we do with voice inflexion or the use of italics in writing. Consider the difference between these three sentences: "I do love you." "Love you, I do." "You do I love." Now, because English operates with different rules, even each of those sentences can have a few implications (and a couple of them sound like Jedi Master Yoda). But Greek, apparently, was a little simpler.

I find this quirk of Biblical Greek intriguing, specifically in Ephesians 4, because it implies a high value on the Evangelist. And though Paul says to the Corinthians that Teachers come after Apostles and Prophets, I believe there is something to the order that Paul uses with the Ephesians. I have friends who have started churches or inherited churches that needed reviving, and a common issue that they have faced is church growth. How do you convince people to come to your new or small church?

Evangelists, that's how. Not only does an Evangelist consistently bring people into the Kingdom, but also they bring them into the church that they go to more often than not. And, as we have discussed, an Evangelist cares deeply about their converts and wants them to come to a church family that is vibrant and inviting. In developing a church, new or growing, one of the primary focuses must be on getting people through the doors. One of the biggest mistakes that leaders make when trying to grow a church is what I call "Sheep Stealing." Instead of building up their people and equipping them to reach out to the world, we spin our wheels trying to be just a little better than the church across the street so that people will come to us instead. We create "inter-church events" to "promote unity in the churches of our city," but in the back of our minds we are hoping that people will change flocks for our greener grass.

Having an official Evangelist will do more to grow a church than perfecting a church service. But more importantly than the Evangelist bringing in new believers each week, the function of the

Evangelist as an official position in a church is to train the people on how to impact the world. Equipping everyone to live the exciting, overflowing, transformational culture of your church outside of the sanctuary and fellowship hall will catapult attendance and corporate momentum to a whole new level. Within the church context, a main Evangelist is the one whose focus is on training and equipping people to live the powerful, dynamic culture of their church and the Kingdom outside their church so that people want what they have. Additionally, they spend time and energy on helping to develop the internal church culture and programs to facilitate the new comers, making the church more attractive and more inviting for outsiders.

By now it has become obvious that this book is less about ministry positions and much more about personality Tribes. So how do the vast majority of Evangelist-Tribe people who are not called to occupational church service live out what burns inside of them? I will tell you, it isn't by casting off the restraints of a career in the world to stand on the street corner and thereby becoming a "fisher of men." In fact, it is quite the opposite. Evangelists are primarily supposed to be outside their church. If that is in Corporate America, wonderful! Access divine favor, obtain and implement divine ideas, and make what you carry so attractive that the world begs to know how to get what you have. Evangelists are the ones who attract others to their churches.

Inside our churches, laity-Evangelists can contribute to helping improve the quality of services, the efficiency of programs, and even the design of the church buildings so that new people won't feel like they have stepped off planet earth and onto planet Whacky in the Swirl-o-verse. Whatever gifts people have can be put to good work in the churches they attend. Essentially, these become deacons of evangelism. Maybe that is by doing Social Media Marketing, but it could also be by seeing a need in the neighborhood and creating a ministry within their church to meet that need. This communicates to the people of the neighborhood that the Church is a place that takes care of its people. It also begs the question, wouldn't you like to be part of a church that is so fulfilled that it has to step off its own property to release the immense pressure built up by the fulfillment and happiness inside?

Pastors

The title of "Pastor" needs some reworking. Do what you will with that. Assuming that an Apostle is leading a church, makes the decisions, and sets the culture, then the responsibility of his Pastor is to steward the corporate heart of the people in that church. This can happen in innumerable ways as it is really a matter of who the Pastor is, what that church's culture is, how big that church is, and any number of other factors. The actual functions and actions are not the important part; the responsibility and focus of the Pastor is what matters.

Whether through sermons or events, the focus of a Pastor is the inspiration and connection of the church members' hearts to the vision and direction of that church. This requires the Pastor to not only be concerned about how the people are doing, but also to be vitally connected to the Apostle and Prophet. Without clear understanding of the heart of the visions, the Pastor will have a difficult time uniting the people's hearts to it. Likewise, without a solid agreement with the direction set by the Prophet, the Pastor will be unable to communicate or council rightly to those who are trying to connect with what their church is doing.

Due to the natures of the Prophet and the Pastor, some of the biggest conflicts can arise here. Yet, when well connected and in relationship, the churches that are most dangerous to the domain of darkness will have strong friendship between these Two. The Prophet and the Pastor are the Two who think about the future the most. Whereas the Prophet is zeroed in on the where their church is going in the future, the Pastor has his or her scope set on how easily the church people will be able to embrace the future. Partnering with each other, these Two have the potential to make their church a safe place, an agile organization, and a flourishing family.

Intercessors are people who are a kind of hybrid between the Pastor and Prophet. They have the foresight of the Prophet and the sensitivity of a Pastor. They don't mind taking time praying with or for people, that is the Pastor-type coming out of them.

One way to identify a Pastor is observing who stays latest after a service, just talking to people, connecting with people, and digging into what they are doing. How we spend our time is an indicator of what we value. However, burnout from being overwhelmed is common with Pastors because it is in their DNA to put others first. Pastors need helpers. It is essential to build a team of Pastor-deacons to take care of the needs of their church congregation members. Pastors, too, are intended to equip the Saints for the work of the ministry. That may look like discipling, but with many churches it looks like establishing a value on their church being a family. The most effective way I have seen this done is through Life Groups.

Whether your church calls them "Life Groups," "Cell Groups," "Home Groups," "Small Groups," or something more creative, the idea is the same. Genuine relational connection does not happen between the parking lot and the pews, it happens when people share life together. Pastors over these groups create a sense of community that adds value to the church experience. You can look back at the Church in the First Century to see how important living life together was to the founding, divinely appointed leaders of the Church.

Teachers

Last, but not least, is the Teacher.

Each of the Five carries part of the puzzle of success for a church. Without each one operating freely and fully, a church can only go so far. The Teacher can play a huge role in putting those pieces together. Far from simply explaining things to people, when fully utilized, the Teacher is the member of the Five that creates the skeletal structure for their church to rely on – through teaching, of course, but also through administration.

As far as the speaking done in a church, the Teacher is the one doing a large portion of the communication and explanation of the vision, the direction, and the inner workings of the church. They are a spokesman for the other leaders of the church, breaking down the details and implications of what is going on.

This is done to help people understand and get on board with their leaders. Teachers help answer hard questions, and are prepared for those questions because they have thought through angles of a situation that most people don't think about.

I was once part of a church that distinguishes between the Head Pastor and a Teaching Pastor. This is very important because the Teaching Pastor was an amazing Teacher. When he teaches, he leads his listeners to conclusions and to questions by the way he teaches, then he answers the questions at the very moment those questions emerge in the hearers' minds. He is a masterful Teacher in his attention to detail and sensitivity to what he says and how he says it. And he is a great leader, but is certainly more Teacher than Pastor. That church has done a great job at placing people in correct positions for their gifting, calling, and personality.

Before I was really in ministry, all I wanted was to speak on stage. I thought, like many of us do, that being a Teacher was the greatest possible life someone could want in ministry. I knew of people who flew all over the world and got paid to teach. People loved to hear them teach so much that they paid for plane tickets and hotels, and even gave them honorariums. What's not to love about that?!

Then I started teaching. And it wasn't what I thought it would be: speaking on small stages, small groups, breakout sessions at conferences, main services at large churches, and even getting flown across the planet to speak! But I realized one very sobering truth: people will believe what you say when you say it in front of a large group.

Exciting when you're young, zealous, and convinced that everything you have to say is both right and important. Sobering when you read what James wrote, "Don't presume to be a teacher, because you will undergo a stricter judgment" (James 3:1). And it only gets more real when you consider that you could easily slip into the category of teachers that Paul warned Timothy about. Paul says, "they want to be teachers, but they don't even know what they are talking about, nor do they understand what they so confidently preach as truth" (1 Timothy 1:7). It hit me that if people believed me simply because I was on stage and had a microphone, or because I was from America or because I was ordained, but I was wrong about something I was teaching, then I was responsible for the consequences of my teaching.

We ought not to desire to be a "Teacher" in the church setting, because in the position of a church's main Teacher, you are responsible to have studied and understood the Scriptures and principles of the Kingdom to the degree that people can trust what you are saying implicitly. Teachers are judged more strictly because of the assumption that people make about the assertions that they make. I have since learned to more frequently say, "as I understand it" or "this is what I think and what I believe, but you need to discover it on your own."

In spiritual matters, it is just as much the job of the Teacher to point people to Jesus, as it is the job of the other Four. It is, however, very difficult for Teachers, at times, because they take so much time and put forth so much effort to understand in order to teach. A subtle arrogance can sneak in and the "oh so wise Teachers" start to draw people to themselves and not to Jesus. This is a dangerous trap that we must avoid at all costs. The judgment that comes to all believers is based on what they have been given. Teachers, who cultivate what they are given, are thus held to a high standard because they are very aware of what they have been given.

In the Church, a Teacher leads by serving the other leaders, making it easy for them to implement their ideas. Teachers lead people by making it easy for them to grasp and integrate into the systems and structures of the community. But they are also responsible to do this in the context of a team, by discipling other Teachers into serving in the same ways. Just like a construction foreman cannot build a house alone, so a Teacher cannot and ought not attempt to guide their church alone.

There are those in church families who do not have an official position, nor do they have the desire to teach from a stage. Others are not naturally very eloquent or have stage fright, but they still identify themselves as a Teacher. These are people who make great Administrative Directors, Managers, and Deacons. They are the people who organize things naturally. They can knock out a to-do list without even trying. They make their church run smoothly by creating structures or systems that just work better than before. They are essential members of a church family and need to be celebrated.

Recognition

In closing this chapter, let's be clear: not everyone is an official Apostle, Prophet, Evangelist, Pastor, or Teacher. That is not to say, however, that there are not driving desires and tendencies within us that look very similar to one of those offices. Being able to associate our mentalities with our Tribe can be liberating and empowering.

The key is to recognize your own Tribe and be excellent at your unique contribution to your church family. Simultaneously, your job is to recognize other people's strengths and Tribes. When we honor, celebrate, and hold each other accountable to the greatness within, we set our Church compass towards Jesus and can run hard into His love for this world.

But this entire chapter applies to a limited group of people. If we are talking about personality categories, then there must be an application in real life. It isn't as if we get saved and get a new personality. So if this whole understanding of the Five cannot help us more fully see people that are not sitting in a pew next to us once a week, then it is incomplete and largely irrelevant. So for those of you wondering when this would apply to your normal person life, read on.

That being said, would you like to hear what happened to the valley city of Haven?

Of course you would. Here is the conclusion of our parable.

The Parable of Ecclon: the Conclusion

Andrew became the mayor of Haven. He led the city for several decades, always seeking to keep Haven feeling like home. Joshua loved to come visit, always encouraging Andrew saying, "Dad would have loved to see what you have created here in Haven." It was easy for the leaders of Fort Follis and Benton to submit to his leadership because he empowered them, made decisions with their input in mind, and trained their children to be the future leaders of Haven. It wasn't long before the names "New Ecclon," "Fort Follis," and "Benton" ceased to be used (or really remembered) by anyone in Haven. No one cared about their old allegiances in light of what Haven had become to them – home.

Piper continued to make her bi-annual trips to Ecclon. At first she would make the trips alone, but as she got older, she had others come with her. Throughout the years there were other natural disasters that were averted because Piper and her friends were able to see the signs earlier and earlier. So Piper started a disaster recognition and response program to train others to do what she had done in the original crisis and in the subsequent years. She never could decide where she wanted to live, so she never had a house in either place. Instead, she lived with Joshua when in Ecclon, and she lived with Andrew when in Haven.

Thatcher founded Benton University. There he taught organizational communication until he handed the presidency of the school over to Patrick's son. Thatcher continued to make Andrew's life easier by innovating more genius plans than the two of them had time to implement. That is, until the two of them retired and handed off all of their responsibilities to their sons.

Evan and Angela never stopped their traveling. Even when Andrew appointed them as co-commissioners of city expansion, they were always finding excuses to leave Haven. Evan and Angela were instrumental in filling Haven, just as they had been in Ecclon. They often brought their staff on trips to cities up and down stream to help the cities flourish – everyone wanted to join their staff. When it came time for them to hand off their position as co-commissioners, they had a hard time choosing from their faithful staff. However, they were excited to give up that responsibility, because that meant one thing to them – more travelling!

Patrick's family never stopped growing. Every child in Haven called him "Papa Patrick". He regularly hosted parties, created city events, and even started a café that never made any profits, because he had a tendency to give away food. On his 80th birthday, the Haven City Council named the fairgrounds and family park after him.

Haven went on expanding, but never lost sight of its roots. In fact, it would not be surprising if Ecclon had been engulfed in the borders of the valley metropolis by now. The people who happen to travel through the valley have always said that, "the people of Haven are the happiest people on earth. No one ever goes hungry, everyone does meaningful work, but also have more fun than imaginable. The children are smart, mature, free, and humble. Their parents live long, look young, and smile without trying."

Sounds familiar, doesn't it?

Out of the Box:
Real Life Application for Dummies

Apostles

As we begin to look at the Five in real life for non-occupational ministers, it will be one of the more difficult parts of this subject to tackle – both as a writer and as one trying to understand this particular revelation. For those who have been around the Church world for any significant amount of time, it is easy to simply tweak our understanding and application inside the church bubble. But taking these perspectives, that largely have "churchy" vocabulary, and applying them on "unholy ground" has proven to be a unique and arduous challenge.

That being said, it is also crucial for us as Christians to have belief and value systems that work universally and not just inside our limited spheres of experience. That goes for our vocabulary, theology, doctrine and our standards of behavior. Paul instructed Timothy to do a background check with people in the world before putting someone in leadership with his churches in Ephesus (1 Timothy 3:7). And with Titus Paul uses the list of virtues commonly used by the secular culture when setting standards for saints, because he knew that if we don't go beyond the world's standards, then they have no reason to embrace our belief system (Titus 1).

Our identity and calling precede our commissioning. What we eventually walk out in life, even our assignment in life, is birthed out of who we are. Discovering our identity is, therefore, a foundational part of fulfilling our calling. In Luke 6 we read about Jesus gathering a crowd and choosing His main 12 disciples. Interestingly, before He ever sent them out to do anything "apostolic," He called them Apostles. This helps us to see that God's intentions for us and His view of us is not contingent upon our response. He gives us our identity and it is up to us to walk it out to whatever degree we choose to do so.

In the real world, it is fairly easy to identify those from the Apostle Tribe. This has somewhat to do with the natural propensity towards leadership. Many CEOs of established and successful companies are Apostles, both by the nature of the position of CEO and by their personality. It takes someone obsessed with culture to run a company. Many CEOs started off as entrepreneurs, which is one of the best examples of an Apostle in non-religious settings. Entrepreneurs are pioneers, visionaries, and innovators. They are the quintessential Apostles in the world.

Just like a good CEO who sets the culture of their company, an athletic team captain is the team Apostle. An NFL team that is strong defensively will likely have a Defensive Line captain that sets a standard of hard work and excellence. A sports team whose owner is more concerned about making money than winning games will have a lot of drama that will keep the media interested, but will not necessarily win championships because the most influential leader has set the value on what makes money. You can identify a team's, a company's, or an organization's Apostle by who has the most influence or sway in the culture of the organization. This does not, however, mean that they are of the Apostle tribe, but simply that they are in a position that lends itself to apostolic people. Therefore, the most effective people in those positions will be from the Apostolic Tribe.

On a larger scale, cultural icons and celebrities are apostolic in that they create culture. The late Steve Jobs, former CEO of Apple, was an Apostle. He created and maintained a culture of technological creativity and innovation within his company, and thereby influenced the global culture. His apostolic nature became more apparent when he died. Apple took some time to really recover. He had been the driving force behind much of the innovation and culture, so his absence was felt immediately. However, like a good leader and a typical Apostle, Steve Jobs set up good leaders that could carry the culture without him. So Apple was able to regain its footing once people saw that the vision of the company was not compromised, people stopped hesitating to invest or buy Apple products.

The nature of Apostles manifests within a company in whatever position they hold. But it is in places of leadership that Apostles shine most brightly. In later chapters we will see how vital it is for people to be in positions within an organization that match their Tribe, for the benefit of the success of the organization. The easiest application to understand for this is in a church context, but it applies across the board.

Prophets

It has been said that if a lie is repeated enough, it becomes the truth. Though Christian beliefs cannot fully agree with the statement, because we know the Truth to be a Man, not an idea, the sentiment is powerful. Particularly in an increasingly relativistic society, the influencers have come to rely on inundation through the media to steer the global culture. It is through the media, especially music, that our generation is fed points of view that become people's perception of truth. We are warned by the Lord to be careful about what we listen to (Mark 4:24 and Luke 8:18); though He was not specifically talking about music, there is no denying that lyrics have great sway on culture.

This was even true in the First Century. Paul quoted a secular poet from the island of Crete named Epimenides when he wrote to Titus (Titus 1:12-13). In a shocking statement, Paul calls Epimenides one of Crete's prophets. Music has a way of breaking into our hearts more easily than most other forms of information transference. Educational psychology discovered long ago that strengthening one's memory of facts is as simple as assigning musical tones in recitation.

How many times have we been putting something in alphabetic order and reverted back to reciting the ABCs Song in our head? My brother memorized the US Presidents by using a song when he was in elementary school and still remembers them as a result. Many of us wouldn't remember every State in the Union if it weren't for that song we were taught in Third Grade. Marketing companies know this all too well, that's why every successful commercial in the 20th Century involved the jingle assigned to product or company.

A young lady from New Zealand named Ella Yelich-O'Connor is an example of a Prophet in the music industry. Known better by her stage name "Lorde," 16-year-old Ella instigated a movement within her generation by writing songs that uncovered the ridiculousness of the typical pop music culture's message while employing the pop music style. In true Prophet fashion, she saw the destructive direction that her generation was being led; she then blew the whistle on the scandalous mentalities being fed to her peers and showed them what she saw as a better way. Steering her peers away from plastic hedonism and towards contentment, her music was received because she spoke the language of pop culture even though she has a decisively anti-pop culture message.

Another musical Prophet in our times is Ben Haggerty, known by his stage name "Macklemore." Like Yelich-O'Connor, Haggerty writes like a Prophet. His breakout single was a song about shopping at a thrift shop instead of buying $50 designer t-shirts. But one of the most striking songs off of his album "The Heist" was a song entitled "Same Love." Haggerty is from Seattle and he proudly descends from an Irish heritage, yet his musical career did not go anywhere near folk music like one might think a proud Irish-American would. Rather, he has ascended in the hip-hop world as a white rapper. "Same Love" is a song endorsing homosexual relationships. In the song Haggerty essentially rebukes his subculture for rejecting gays.

Now, I am not endorsing Macklemore, Haggerty's message, or homosexuality. What I am saying, however, is that Haggerty is an example of a Prophet to the hip-hop music community and subculture. He witnessed something that he viewed as hazardous to his community and used his influence and giftedness to attempt to shift the culture. This is what Prophets do, for good or in error. It doesn't matter; they are shifters and sculptors of culture. Whether it is correcting the mentalities of youthful materialism or attempting to help a marginalized people group gain acceptance, or any number of other examples, musicians are voices to each generation.

Other examples of Prophets in the non-religious world are business analysts and consultants. They troubleshoot potential problems, foresee the current direction of businesses, and give suggestions to CEOs about how to avoid or get out of current problems. Also political activists, small party politicians and bloggers can be Prophets in that they see current problems with how the government is presently operating and are unwilling to keep quiet about it. This is a sign of a Prophet; even if they don't have a position to speak from, they will urgently present their perspective – and their position is not necessarily being spoken from God's perspective. Like Jeremiah, the message or perspective that they are carrying is like a fire shut up inside of them that they are unable to contain (Jeremiah 20:9). Prophets will do just about anything to get their opinion heard, no matter how uncomfortable or unpopular.

The Libertarian political party is a fairly poignant example of this. Do not view this as a political endorsement, but merely an observation that has application to what we are looking at in this book. The obsession of the Libertarian Party is the United States Constitution, and in much of their speeches, marketing and media, the overwhelming message is a call to return to the Constitution and values upon which our nation was founded. As you would expect from a Prophet, most Libertarian politicians sound like revolutionaries – prepared to make radical, extreme changes in order to avoid an imminent national doom.

This can be one of the most controversial aspects of this book for good reason: Prophets are many times the most controversial of the Five. Both in the Church and in the world, Prophets always call for change. They bring correction to hazardous direction. Embracing one's Prophetic Tribe takes courage and support, because it is not an easy life as a trumpeter when first the perception is that the Prophet is a bringer of bad news – especially when that Prophet knows that change is the good news if it is accepted.

Evangelists

The Evangelist, Pastor and Teacher are generally more like managers and don't get as much acclaim or visibility. Thus, examples are less specific in terms of big, recognizable names.

That is not to say that they are not leaders by any means, but rather that they do their leading in less conspicuous ways and are less in the public eye than the first two. Each has its benefits and challenges.

Evangelists are inspirers. They are the people that are always telling you about the new thing; a new CD, a new movie, a new technology, they are the unofficial spokesmen of the New. They are excited about something and they let people know every chance they get. They are the underground music enthusiasts, the viral social media people, and the kind of people that you get around who make life more interesting, exciting and vibrant – though sometimes a bit messier as well.

Evangelists make incredible marketers. They instinctively know how to reach people, draw people in, and inspire them. And like a church Evangelist does for a church, Evangelists in the world don't just bring in people, they also have a keen sense of how to retain people. They know their audience really well and can be experts on customer retention, because they are in tune with how outsiders work.

They also make great salesmen. They have a knack for reading people and helping them get on board with something new. Whether it is a new product presentation at a board meeting, advertising a service, or something as simple as getting the company Scrooge to attend the company Christmas party, Evangelists nuzzle themselves into people's hearts and influence them by appealing to people as a friend. Have you ever watched an infomercial and felt like the product's spokesman wasn't trying to sell you something, but they were actually trying to help you? Their life was transformed by this product and they genuinely want you to experience the same revolution in your life.

Evangelists in the world make friends really easily. You feel like you are the most important person they have ever met. You are drawn into who they are and their life inspires your heart to ask the question, "What is it that makes their life so good? I've got to find out." Their honesty and genuine nature, even if you saw them on TV or at a large meeting, makes you feel like you could just go start a real conversation with them like you would with a childhood friend. You trust them easily and are pulled into their wake (without complaint).

Again, it is hard to point to a cultural icon as an example, but particularly for the Evangelist, because the essence of an Evangelist is that of pointing people towards something or someone else. Evangelists get a lot of attention, but they aren't looking for it. In fact, Evangelists get a lot of satisfaction out of people taking their advice. Sometimes celebrities will act like Evangelists by promoting a good cause. They use their position to call people to action on clean water for African children, renewable energy, political activism, or some other entity that they see as worthy of their endorsement. But a true Evangelist is not a glory hog, they are pretty selfless and looking to promote others and point people towards greater fulfillment in life.

Pastors

By now, having read this far in the book, you are probably starting to anticipate what I'm going to say about each of the Five because you are getting a grid for each of the Five. If that is the case, you may automatically equate the Pastor with being a professional counselor. That very well might be a great place for a Pastor. Therapists certainly would need to have a pastoral bent and value the movements of the heart. But it is broader than that. Sometimes the Human Relations staff at a company has to be pastoral. Though they are largely administrative, which is the stomping ground of the Teacher, people are cared for by the Human Relations staff.

You run into Pastors every day. They are your kids' favorite teacher in school, who takes the extra time make sure their students aren't overwhelmed by homework. The most memorable athletic coaches that I had in middle school and high school were the ones who didn't relate to me solely based on my performance numbers on the field, but who would pull me into their office and ask me how I was doing at home because they could tell I was upset. They were being a Pastor to me, caring for my heart and laying down their lives for my benefit.

Think of the bosses or managers who you have had. There is likely one that sticks out in your mind. One that you actually enjoyed working for or who really made you feel important in your job, and therefore you really wanted to work for them. They quite possibly could have been a Pastor. They didn't treat you like a work horse or a robot that made their job easier, they let you leave work early because it had been a stressful day and they wanted you to be at peace. Or maybe you have had a boss that corrected you in something you were doing wrong, but after the confrontation you could feel that they really wanted you to improve as a person, not as an employee. They saw the gold in you, and they expected you to manifest your greatness.

I'm not much of a TV watcher, and generally I do not think that daytime talk shows are worth a person's time, but I see it as a great outlet for a Pastor to not only talk to individuals about their problems but also to help viewers to engage their hearts in compassion. It is even a way for a Pastor to demonstrate how to care for someone's heart. Viewers can see how to help their friends, thus the host is actually discipling the viewers in pastoring. Additionally, in viewing a Pastor at work in caring for someone's heart, it helps viewers to engage their hearts and get the same kind of care vicariously.

When a calamity or crisis occurs in the United States, it is assumed that the President will make a national address about what is happening and what the plan is to rectify the situation. This is the Presidential duty as a type of Pastor to the nation. The purpose of these presidential addresses is not dissemination of information, the purpose is to quell the fears of the people by showing them that there are people that are defending their safety and freedom.

While the media may paint law enforcement officers in a bad light, there are plenty of friendly local police officers – a vast majority, I would argue. Most police officers do not go into training academy thinking, "I just want to get a gun and be able to legally shoot bad guys." The heart behind law enforcement is "to serve and protect." That might as well be the mantra of the Pastor. In fact, one of my mentors in my twenties, who was one of the most Pastoral people I have ever known, was not just a policeman – he was a SWAT team sniper. He told me once about the time he came closest to actually having to shoot a man as a sniper. He said he was praying for his target the entire time he had the perpetrator in his crosshairs. He wanted that guy to be free and alive. He also told me about officers who developed friendships with people they had arrested. They would check up on them to make sure they were doing well. That changed my view of police officers forever.

Teachers

Just because someone teaches, that does not necessarily mean they are a Teacher. Occupationally, educators do get paid to teach, but their approach to people may be drastically different from a Teacher as we are discussing them. An occupational teacher could be any of the Five. As we laid out in the chapter on the Teacher earlier, Teachers are dynamic thinkers and visionary planners. They are instrumental in constructing the skeleton of a culture by creating systems of understanding and operation that will support the community they are serving. They are the people that you first think of when you "just need to get the thing done, and done quickly, but done right." However, a Teacher is not the one you want to lead it ultimately.

Many times I have seen Administrative Assistants are in the Teacher Tribe. They can think of really creative and easy ways to accomplish what is needed for the organization they are working for. The most dynamic set up I have ever seen was when two Teachers worked with each other. One was the director of a department at a non-profit on the East Coast, the other was his Administrative Assistant. Because they were both Teachers, they both thought about great ways of doing things, organizing and implementing projects. It was brilliant to watch them work together.

You may have run into Teachers in real life and didn't even see it. Like the mechanic or plumber who sees the problem that you called them about and refuses to take payment from you because it is a simple fix that you can do yourself with their instruction. They take so much delight in showing you and empowering you to do the fix yourself, that they don't mind losing out on the financial benefit.

Engineers tend to be Teachers. They love learning, figuring out how things work, coming up with solutions, and innovating better ways of doing things. City planners, IT guys, and project managers tend to be Teachers in that they are solution oriented, creative, intelligent, and get excited about the creation process. As you would expect, it is hard to come up with specific examples of famous Teachers because real, true Teachers don't get a lot of time in the spotlight. For Teachers, it isn't about giving out information. For them, enjoyment and fulfillment comes from the creation of dynamic, effective systems that make things work in such a way that you don't realize the system or structure is in place. The success of the innovation is praise enough for the Teacher.

I Need You, But You Drive Me Crazy: Honoring The Other Four

Stay in Your Lane: Being "You" is Not My Job

If you have ever driven a car in a country outside of America and most European nations, where there are far fewer traffic laws, road signs, and other driving assumptions, you know just how important it is to have established rules for transportation. Having lanes makes a big difference in the flow of traffic. When construction reduces the number of available lanes, traffic goes slow, tempers get hotter, and accidents become more frequent. And when someone does not stay in their lane, whether by swerving or intentionally changing lanes, it isn't long before someone snaps.

In every type and size of organization, from families to Fortune 500s, it is important that people "stay in their lane." It is not the job of the mail distributor to make decisions on corporate mergers. And many times if a CEO tries to make suggestions about how the blue-collar workers do something, it is generally unrealistic, uninformed, and unhelpful. If everyone does what is inside of them to do, the whole will do much better and the individual will be much happier.

In most cases, it is even counterproductive to have an opinion outside of one's own lane. Consider the mail distributor, if they have a strong opinion about the corporation's website design, what good does that opinion do? Or what if a Senator walks into a Post Office in a small town and tries to make suggests about how they run the place, though he was only coming to buy stamps? Granted, he likely has a history of great leadership and problem solving; but the Post Office is not his primary realm of authority or expertise. His opinions, even if it is correct, will prove to be agitating to the Post Master who has been working there for three decades. Remaining in our own lane in how we act and in what we think can save us, and those around us, a substantial amount of stress and frustration.

Sometimes in the ambiguity of an organization, particularly small organizations where people wear multiple hats, a subtle pressure crops up to do more than we are supposed to do. Whether that is to stay on our bosses' good side, "not let down the team" or self-made pressure rooted in a Messiah complex, it is crucial to stick to our particular responsibilities. This is prevalent in ministries; everyone is expected to do pastoral ministry, even if they are gifted in administration or called to some other area of the ministry.

It is not my job to be you. It is not your job to be me. I must do my part and you must do yours, otherwise one of us is obsolete. This goes for denominations as well. Charismatic churches are not primarily meant to do what the Baptist, the Catholics, or the Methodists do. Each has its place and purpose in the body. We do not need three arms on the Body of Christ, we need two; if a leg tries to be an arm, then the whole body will fall over.

If you identify most with the Prophet, do not give into the pressure to be pastoral just because the community you are in places a high value on Pastors. If you are a Teacher, but you see a need for an Apostolic person to step into their role as leader...keep teaching. Your community needs you to teach well. If someone is pressuring you to be something that isn't in you to be, stand strong in who you really are. The right person will be drawn to that place to fulfill that need. Your presence in a wrong position keeps the right person from being able to fill their purpose, as well as keeps you from fully entering into your purpose where you are supposed to be.

Giving and Receiving Grace: General Principle of Healthy Happiness

Having read the descriptions of the Five, and taking other personality tests, you will be better equipped to understand the people around you. If you want to live in healthy happiness, it is good practice to give grace to everyone around you. This does not mean to just let things go. It means understanding people, non-judgmentally evaluating their strengths, and being aware of their weaknesses. Then you can treat and honor them rightly.

Albert Einstein said, "Everybody is a genius. But if you judge a fish by its ability to climb a tree, it will live its whole life believing that it is stupid." Physiologically speaking, in the Body of Christ analogy, if we expect an ear to see, we will be disappointed. Or if we demand the brain to do anything except process the signals that come to it, we will consider it worthless. But if we appreciate the ear for its ability to enjoy music, hear things that the rest of the body cannot perceive, and even aid in the equilibrium of the body, then we can use it most effectively. Like when we need to escape into a good song, we will know to whom we can turn – our good friend the ear. And when we are in the pitch dark and can't tell where we are, we can embrace our ear's uncanny ability to pick up on what our eye is unable to perceive in the dark. But if we do not appreciate it, as anyone who has ever had vertigo will tell you, it is nearly impossible for the rest of the body to function when it cannot tell which direction is down.

Riding the Median: A Systematic Breakdown of Wrong-Lane-ness

By now, you should have an idea of which of the Five you more closely identify with, if you did not already know. The following is a generalized but systematic breakdown of what happens with each of the Five when forced to function in someone else's lane. Since most people who will read this book will be Christians, I will tend to frame it more in a corporate church context to help with a framework. But all of these find their best application in the context that our life happens to land us. Whether that is a church, Non-Profit Organization, business, or a large family, the principle still holds true.

I encourage you to not just read the section that applies to you. In reading each scenario, try to think of an instance when you have seen these principles played out. This will give you an appreciation for being in the right place and position and give you compassion for those around you who are not rightly positioned.

If an Apostle tries to be…

… a Prophet:

An Apostle is inherently stubborn for the culture that they are carrying to create. If they are put in the position of a Prophet in a community, they will bring correction and direction based on culture that they carry. This will seem to those expecting a Prophet that they are never bringing a "new word," because the Apostle is not interested in something new but in creating and maintaining a culture.

… an Evangelist:

An Apostle is a builder, not a gatherer. So when treated like an Evangelist, an Apostle will feel like they are "spinning their tires" and get bored with not building anything. Eventually they will start to build a community, and will be viewed as rebellious and insubordinate, and their leaders will be frustrated with them for not being "all in with us." They are designed to be a major pillar in a community that they are in leadership over, not a gatherer bringing others to someone else's vision for a community.

…a Pastor:

The visionary nature of an Apostle can severely affect the way that they relate to those they are leading. Whereas Pastors in a church setting are expected to be very personable, kind, individually engaging, and sensitive, many times it is just not in an Apostle to spend time on the "heart minutiae" demanded of Pastors. They will glaze over when someone starts opening up their heart and seem impatient when "superficial" or "unimportant life issues" are being talked about. And the Apostle will know that they cannot live up to the expectations put on them and feel like a failure or a jerk.

...a Teacher:

I suspect this is a very common situation in our churches in America. Many Apostles lead churches as their "pastor" and therefore do the bulk of the teaching on Sunday mornings. Their sermons are nebulous idealism that leave the congregation feeling like they need to change something, but don't really know what to change or how to change. Or maybe their teaching is impractical vision-casting, and because it is so ethereal, the congregation feels very inspired about what they heard but do not know how to apply it to their lives. This leaves the people inspired and the Apostle discouraged because the people feel the epic nature of the created culture, but they need a Teacher to show them how to walk it out in real life.

If a Prophet tries to be...

...an Apostle:

The simple reality is that some people are wired to create culture and others are wired to improve culture. A Prophet is best at sculpting culture and shifting its direction so that it does not hit a snag or become stagnant. The culture that a Prophet will create could seem unstable to those in their community. This is not because a Prophet is a critical or unstable person, but because their purpose is to change things for the better. Being an Apostle requires an innate reference point to emulate and a vision to recreate that culture. A Prophet is a creative thinker that is more of a "tweaker" than an initiator. A Prophet will optimistically keep moving towards a goal, but the culture could struggle to settle down or lock into a corporate identity.

...an Evangelist:

Wrong target. Wrong purpose. A Prophet is oriented towards the whole culture, not individuals. A Prophet is supposed to shift culture, not gather people to the culture. And many times a Prophet does the opposite of gathering people – people don't like change, generally. This misplacement is a recipe for a lot of pressure to mess with everyone involved.

...a Pastor:

Built into the heart of a Prophet is an obsession with the future. When someone is expecting a Prophet to be "pastoral," they will feel like the Prophet is being harsh or cold. Rather than focusing on feeding the sheep, they are more concerned about how the sheep chew or what the cost of sheep food is going to be next quarter. They want to correct the sheep to make them receive the food better, or correct the Teacher for not thinking ahead and planning on getting feeding troughs that won't rust out. They still care about the sheep, but more conceptually than practically or individually.

...a Teacher:

Imagine trying to get somewhere important and urgent, but having no map, no GPS and no directions, just being told what the destination looks like. That is what a Prophet would do in a Teacher's position. Their focus on the end goal and distaste for administrative details keeps them from effectively helping people traverse the valley between current location and ultimate destination. Both the Prophet and the people will be frustrated as the Prophet expects them to just get it and figure it out for themselves, and the people are trying to ask how, why, when, and where they are going.

If an Evangelist tries to be...

...an Apostle:

Though these Two are very close in their personalities, at the heart of an Evangelist, they are excited about the community they are connected to and want to bring people there. However, an Apostle needs to create and maintain a new community's culture. An Evangelist will end up inspiring people to go back to the place that they were sent from; rather than recreating the culture of Ecclon in New Ecclon, like an Apostle would, they would make people want to move to Ecclon more than settle in New Ecclon. The Evangelist will more likely than not feel in over their head.

...a Prophet:

Evangelists are essentially marketers. They are really good at broadcasting the Good News, drawing people towards the culture that they are representing, but they are wired to affect a community by bringing in new people. An Evangelist, like the Pastor and Teacher, are supposed to affect a certain part of the community's culture – they believe that their part is the *most* important part. As a result, the effect of their attempts at culture shifting will be telling people to do what they are supposed to be doing. This will feel like shaming and condemning. This is a good kind of myopia that is beneficial in the Evangelist, Pastor and Teacher, which will cause them to do their part with excellence. But a Prophet must be able to view the whole community and sculpt the parts of the whole in the direction that the culture is shifting.

...a Pastor:

If a Pastor is a shepherd, an Evangelist is rancher. Their job is to corral the sheep into the correct pen, but once they are in the correct field the rancher is done. The sheep can take care of themselves now that they are out of the dangerous areas and are now where they can feed, mate, sleep safely, and do whatever sheep do. A shepherd lives with the sheep and takes it upon himself to make sure they all grow up healthy. An Evangelist in a Pastor's position will likely get overwhelmed with the details, drama, and decisions connected to caring for the people.

...a Teacher:

Like an Evangelist in a Pastor's position, an Evangelist will get bogged down in the administration, planning and details that a Teacher revels in. They will feel out of place because they want to draw people into the community so that the Pastors and Teachers can take care of them – that's just how they are wired.

If a Pastor tries to be...

...an Apostle:

As we have seen, Pastors' main focus is the hearts of the people in a community. Specifically, how the hearts of the people in a community connect to the vision and direction of the community. Now, if the leader of a community is naturally inclined towards people's hearts, the culture of that community will be people oriented. This could lead to the culture remaining comfortable for the masses. This is where we get unhealthy, extreme "seeker" churches that care more about people enjoying the community than standing on the Word of God and taking the ground they are called to take. Also the requirements of creating and maintaining a culture can overload a Pastor who cares mostly about people's heart health.

...a Prophet:

In a church setting, a Pastor being asked to correct and direct a community will tend to give "soft correction." Rather than actually helping the culture to steer clear of future obstacles, not wanting to offend or alienate anyone, a Pastor may continue to encourage everyone. Though everyone was having a great night on the Titanic, hundreds died because the alarm was not sounded in time. Being concerned with people's feelings can hinder a Prophet's function, but it is exactly what a Pastor is meant to carry.

...an Evangelist:

A Pastor loves to care for sheep. It is in their DNA. So when they are expected to go gather sheep, they will feel out of place and will not feel comfortable sending those they gather to someone else to be taken care of; they got to know them to bring them in, and they are best suited to help them. This is where we get "The Church of St. Arbucks," where true Pastors went and collected wild sheep and didn't have a place they felt comfortable sending them. So they meet weekly in a coffee shop and the Pastor stops gathering and starts shepherding, because that is who he is, and that's what he does. This is not rebellion; it is a misplaced assignment.

...a Teacher:

This is such a common issue in the American church. Where a Teacher is meant to help the minds of the community connect with the vision, the Pastor is meant to help the hearts. A "teaching sermon" on a Sunday morning by a true Pastor will be more focused on answering the heart objections that may crop up in the congregation than on creating a framework for the congregation's mind to understand and function within. Both the leader and the followers will feel the misfiring but may not know what is wrong in the engine.

If a Teacher tries to be...

...an Apostle:

A Teacher's soul burns with a passion for dynamic systems that work well. The problem comes when a Teacher is expected to create and maintain a culture, what they will create is a solid community that is oriented towards the systems, dynamic guidelines and rules. Though this will be a well-organized community, the heart of the community will feel empty. The Teacher does what they do really well, but the vision is lacking and the means becomes the end goal. This subtle, unintentional pressure is what we like to call "religion."

...a Prophet:

Teachers *love* details. So a Teacher whose function in a community is to sculpt and shift the culture will correct minor details. These may be things that really do need to be changed, but the Prophet's task in a community is the direction of the community. A Teacher viewed as a Prophet will seem "nitpicky" and will seem to "miss the forest while looking at the trees."

...an Evangelist:

Strictly in a church setting, a Teacher that is expected to evangelize will argue people into an apologetic salvation. Those that they convert will be convinced of the practical reasons for coming to the Teacher's church. In the rest of the world, a Teacher would go crazy trying to organize things they are not in control of because their realm of influence and authority does not stretch outside of their community. And then there is the issue of trying to impose structures that work in one community on others in order to draw them into that community...it just doesn't work. Structures are meant to help maintain a culture, but no matter how dynamic our systems, people are drawn by passion, vision, and relationship, not programs.

...a Pastor:

This is another very common set-up in the American church. Someone with a great ability to explain, who has a passion to learn deep truths and teach them is put in the lead position at a church. They call him the Senior Pastor, but the guy couldn't counsel his way out of a wet paper bag. The issue is that Teachers are meant to solve problems, so if a person comes with a "pastoral issue," they see them as a project to complete and not a sheep to lead. Discipleship becomes a consultation briefing when it needs to be more like a massage therapy session for their soul. Follow up meetings become frustrating when the "pastor" asks if they applied the principles given in the last meeting and week after week the answer is an ashamed, "no."

Demanding Greatness: Honor By Expecting Me to Live My Identity

When I was a child, my parents treated my brother and me like adults as early as I can remember. In varying degrees, they would give us greater and greater personal responsibility and freedom to make our own decisions. I do not remember a single meal that my parents said, "this is what we are eating, like it or not." They always gave us a choice and asked us what we wanted to eat. This matured us quickly. Our parents expected us to act like adults, so we did.

For a few years, I was a pastor at MorningStar University. In my discipleship of the students, I tried to take this same strategy in counseling and conflict resolution. I determined in my heart to see the students for who they were becoming, not for who they presently were. This called them up to the next level. I constantly told students to act in the present like who they are becoming. The ones who took this advice grew exponentially faster than they had been growing because they began to see themselves in finished form, not caught in the junk they were bound to in the moment.

This principle of behavioral expectation is rooted in honor. It is calling the real you to manifest regardless of the circumstances. Like the Lord did to Gideon, who certainly was not easily labeled a "mighty warrior," we can use our words to "honor someone into their destiny." We speak into being the things that are not yet manifesting. Jesus expected the fig tree to produce fruit even when it was not the season for figs. The standard and expectation of Grace is actually higher than the standard that the regulations of the Law try to produce in us. Jesus expected supernatural things out of natural circumstances.

When you know that I am an Apostle, called to create and maintain a culture, and see me acting contrary to that, the best thing you can do for me is to confront me with my true identity and calling. This snaps me out of my temporary insanity and propels me into repentance (the changing of how I think, and thereby the way I act). When we operate in our true identity, we carry a reward with us for those who receive us rightly. A Prophet received as a Prophet gives the receiver a prophetic reward, but if received otherwise the Prophet will only be able to bless the receiver according to how they are received.

Of course we have seen this done wrongly when someone has an unreasonable expectation of us. In many of those situations, the poison is present in that relationship because the one with unreasonable expectations is demanding those things for their own personal benefit, not the benefit of the one they are holding to a higher standard. When we demand greatness out of someone, it must be because that is their identity, not because it will benefit us or other people.

Jesus demanded figs of a fig-less tree, and when it did not respond to the Voice of its Creator, He cursed it (Mark 11). Jesus rebuked the Pharisees, saying that if people would not praise Him, the rocks would praise Him (Luke 19:40). Paul handed a man over to the devil so that this man could eventually be redeemed (1 Corinthians 5:5). This expectation of greatness can let something die fully so that it can be resurrected. From the dead fig tree, another more fruitful tree could grow in its place. People are His preferred source of worship, but He is not needy towards humanity to get His "worship fix." If Paul did not rightly judge the man in Corinth, he could have been trapped in a religiously toxic environment that would not force him into a decision point where he would fully turn and repent.

God is not under pressure, nor does He pressure us, but He does invite all of us to incalculable greatness. What determines our level of greatness in this age and the age to come is our level of agreement with His opinion of us. Will we lean into who He has made us to be? Or will we shrink back from our exceedingly high calling and label it "humility"?

Humility: Making Room for Me by Saying "NO" to Things That Don't Fit Me

True humility is agreeing with God's opinion. It is not pride for me to walk up to a chimpanzee and confidently state in its face, "I am made in the image of God, and you are not." Nor is it arrogance to say confidently that I am a Prophet, despite the fact that my life may not reflect that assertion. In both cases, they are seminal truths that need development and maturity, for I am not a perfect reflection of His image, nor am I a mature Prophet with the office and influence that one day I will have.

This is an identity issue that effects how we live our lives. If we are supposed to be a prophetic voice to our community, we should not be tied up with pastoral meetings. Likewise, if you are a pastor, called to shepherd the hearts of junior high students, and you are asked to teach at a conference, you must only take that opportunity if the Lord directs you to. Our assignment in the Lord is the most important thing we can give ourselves to, everything that pulls us away from that is a distraction that will derail us.

Some people could take this too far and think that I am saying that someone with a "high calling" can neglect and even reject menial tasks that they simply do not want to do. But I will heartily bring to remembrance that Jesus said that the greatest among us will be the servant of all (Matthew 23:11). He proceeded to take the position of the very lowest slave in the building and washed the disciples' nasty, stinking, sweaty feet (John 13). But I want to also point out that there was a moment when those same disciples were serving people so much in physical ways that they were unable to serve them in the way they could best – in prayer and the ministry of the Word (Acts 6).

It was not arrogance for them to say, "we can't keep working in the soup kitchen, we need to pray and preach." It was supreme humility, because they saw that they could be best used at that time by operating in their callings as apostles. They had already been showing people how to live kingdom-style (serving), but they had to make the transition to oversight now that the culture of the Kingdom had caught on. They were also diligent to put people in their place so that there wasn't a gaping hole from their absence.

It takes real humility to say "no" to things that look like great opportunities but are distractions. But it also takes courageous humility to say "no" to things that do not fit your calling that people consider "below" you, because people will think that your act of humility is actually an act of arrogance. Such a tricky balance, isn't it? But the Apostles gave us a good model in Acts 6 – serve like crazy where you are until the Lord shows you a more effective way for you to serve. If you know that God has given you a teaching gift, it is not humility for you to neglect that gift to scrub toilets when the Lord has provided you the opportunity to teach.

Turn this all around. Take it off yourself. We mustn't let those around us do things that they are not equipped and called to. If I see a true Teacher it is my responsibility to promote them, even…dare I say it?...give them *my* place to teach. If I do not serve them and the community in this way, I promote anemic body life. Lifeless bodies begin to stink. This begins by being rightly related to each part of the Body and celebrating their gifts, talents, callings, and personalities.

From Tolerance to Appreciation: Relating To The Other Four

From (not so) Secret Irritation to Celebration: A Change of Heart

It is inevitable that as we live in community with people, we will "rub each other wrong" at times. If the Lord just wanted us to get saved and whisk us off to Heaven, He would send a few really good preachers into the world to get people to say "yes" to Him and then yank them up to Heaven – by death or rapture. But salvation is a process that involves not only Justification (the removal of the *penalty* of sin) but also Sanctification (the removal of the *power* of sin in our lives) and Glorification (the removal of the *presence* of sin at the Second Coming). Sanctification is the process that we go through during our days in the Kingdom leading up to our death or His Coming. And, like it or not, that process requires OTHER PEOPLE. We need other people to be the iron that sharpens us and smoothes out our rough edges.

Most of the time the Lord delivers us of internal bondage using external circumstances. Specifically, He uses the rest of His Body to help highlight where we are off or where we are not rightly relating to Him or His Body. And generally we keep our irritation with people secret. If we are mature and wise, we recognize our need for freedom when we manifest irritation with other people and release it to the Lord. But sometimes we are not so secretive about our irritation with other people, and the Lord helps us in those cases to get free in other ways. In fact, He gets as many people freed up through these kinds of circumstances as He possibly can.

But all of the friction is rooted, for the most part, in not being rightly joined to the other parts of the Body. Knowing our own identity and purpose is only half of the battle; we also need to know those with whom we labor so that we cannot just tolerate them, but celebrate them and be in right relationship to them. It does a hand only so much good to realize it is a hand. In order to remain alive and function rightly and effectively, the hand must find a wrist and connect to it. And though an ankle looks similar to a wrist, a hand will only function at partial potential in a foot's place. A hand is meant to be used for different things and is designed to be used for a "higher" calling.

In order to move forward, we need a change of heart. We need to celebrate each other's purpose and identity in addition to acknowledging and embracing our own. The next few sections will help in this process. We will look at how each of the Five relates best with the other Four. The purpose of these is not to give us ammo to shoot at others for mistreating us, but to help us understand our ways of relating to and celebrating the strengths of the others.

If we really lean into this, we will actually start to enjoy people that previously drove us crazy. Trust me, I have seen it and lived it. As soon as I realized who I am and recognized who others are, I suddenly had grace for them and figured out how to help them have grace for me. This has helped friends of mine to have patience in the process of becoming a healthy community with a truly dynamic culture.

Let me reiterate a warning: This is not to help point the finger at others, showing that they are doing something wrong. Even the Scriptures are not meant for that, though we can tend to use them for that. When we read the Scriptures that focus on Christian behavior, if our first and primary response is not to look at our own lives and see how fully we are living up to the Scriptural standard set before us in the New Testament, then we join the ranks of the Pharisees. And like the Pharisees, we will put heavy loads on people that we are not ourselves able to carry (Matthew 23:4). Our disciples will become doubly demonized, or "twice the sons of hell as yourselves" as Jesus put it, because they will be confused and condemned (Matthew 23:15).

As you read these next sections, apply it to *your* life, *your* actions, and *your* attitudes first. Once you have mastered that, then you can cast the first stone at those that are not doing it. But I suspect that if you go through the process of reorienting your thoughts towards others (a.k.a. repentance), you will know how it feels to be freed by this process and you will not judge others, but you will look to help them experience the freedom you have walked into through this process. So take Jesus' advice, and mine, and take care of the tree trunk in your eye, then you can see well enough to help your friends with the sawdust in their eyes (Matthew 7:3). As an added bonus, you will keep yourself from whacking those you love in the head with the telephone pole in your eye as you try to "help" them…not helpful.

How an Apostle Relates to the Other Four

If you are an Apostle, you are a hub of culture. If you have ever studied leadership or been in leadership (very likely if you are an Apostle), then you know that leadership is mostly about serving those you are leading. The actions of those under a leader do not normally serve the leader as much as most people think. It is your responsibility to lead, but it is also your burden to bear.

As you relate to Prophets, stay flexible to the changes that they are called to bring to the culture you are stewarding. This will be difficult because you have created this thing and it can become part of who you are, but realize that they love the community too. They are doing their part. They are wired to see the future and prepare for it. The changes they are proposing are not attacks on you. They will be responsible for the correction and direction that they propose just like you are responsible for the creation and maintenance of the culture. Trust them, but also trust God *in* them.

When relating to the Evangelist, Pastor, and Teacher, it is vital that you make sure they know that you value them. If they are your subordinates, they are not your slaves. You have the helm, but if they do not do their job the boat will not move – at least not for very long. Give them priority with your time and energy and resources, for they are the ones that will ultimately make the culture you are trying to create work or fail.

With Evangelists, be sure that they know what you are creating. If they advertise one thing outside of your community that is inaccurate, the people they bring in will expect what the Evangelist told them and be disappointed. Make sure to keep them connected to the community. Lead them, value them, encourage them, and don't let them drift off into La-La-Land. Honor them in front of other leaders for their contribution to the community and reward them for their hard work. Paul told Timothy to pay double salary to those who do work (preaching and teaching specifically) inside and outside his church (1 Timothy 5:17). If you have an Evangelist that is effective on both sides of the walls of your church, let it show in their bank account.

If anyone is going to have a real finger on the pulse of the community, it is the Pastor. As an Apostle, do not get so stuck in vision of the culture that you forget that the culture is about *people*. The Pastor will know how the sheep are doing; don't use them to get your vision accomplished, but honor them as the barometer of the community. Give them the freedom to spend time with people. They are your watchmen, your overseers, and they are the ones that are most willing to get down and dirty with the real heart issues of the community that you don't have time for. Let them use their gift of dealing with people by sending them people to disciple, but also set them up for success by watching out for them. They will by nature lay down their lives for people, but they will forget to take breaks and will burn themselves out if you don't pastor your Pastor.

Ask any pilot how important a great engineer is to flight. If it were not for the Teacher, your vision would stay in idea form and never materialize. Make sure your Teachers know what the Prophets have shifted in the direction of the community, because the Teacher is the one who will make it happen. They will see the technical big picture just like you see the visionary big picture. The earlier they know, the better. They are wired to make things happen, but you will need to have patience and grace for them as they tackle the challenges of conveying vision and direction to the people in a practical manner. Don't micro-manage them. Trust them, but more importantly, include them in most of what you are thinking. They are very practical and will thrive to the degree that they are trusted and honored.

When I first started teaching on relating to other personalities, I didn't include how to relate to people like yourself. It never occurred to me that like-minded people could have conflict. But the more I have looked at it, the more I came to see that two or more of any two of the Five in one community can cause friction – just as much friction as between the others. If you encounter another Apostle, do not be threatened by them or get into competition with them. The best thing you can do is celebrate what they are called to do and encourage them to do their thing well – it will accelerate your growth as well. Avoid trying to add what they are doing to your calling. Stay in your lane. Like we saw with trying to be another of the Five, trying to be an Apostle in someone else's way is equally as detrimental. On paper, Paul would have been a better apostle to the Jews, but God sent him to the Gentiles and sent Peter to the Jews. God knows the best assignment for you; that is why He gave it to *you*.

How a Prophet Relates to the Other Four

If you are a Prophet, your concern in your community is the movement and direction of the culture. It can be a hard assignment to have, because you are supremely aware of hindrances, but you love your community and want to see it succeed. I know that. You know that. Others do not necessarily recognize that. So it is your responsibility to reassure everyone else that you are excited and hopeful about the awesome future of your community...but still serve the community by helping to avoid the pitfalls on the road ahead. You can see the pitfalls easily; that is your gift and your burden. Serve everyone with it, and don't worry about if they believe you. Be faithful to what you are being shown.

Apostles and Prophets are partners. They have to trust and honor one another. As you relate to the Apostle of your community, honor is going to be the lubrication in your relationship. Friction is inevitable, but you can reduce it by treating the Apostle with honor. They started the community; before God they are responsible for the decisions that are made in the culture. You are there to help the Apostle get to the destination. Never come with condescension or even a hint of superiority. It will shut down your voice in the ear of the Apostle. The Apostle has laid down their life to create this culture. Help them accomplish it by coming humbly and serving as a long-distance watchman.

As you partner with the Apostle, you will find that you have to relate to the Evangelists, Pastors, and Teachers similarly to how the Apostle does. You are both high-vision in your perspective, which means that you need the other Three to take what you are seeing and make it practical. Honor them in how you talk about them and how you talk with them. Encourage them and communicate with them often. This will make your job more enjoyable and their jobs easier.

Specifically, with an Evangelist, you will see what will be most effective for them before they do. Be a consistent voice in their lives that helps them to avoid traps and fruitless endeavors, both in their position and their personal life. This will create a culture within the community of trust and promote an atmosphere of safety. The people that they bring in will be much easier for you to shift and lead, so the more effective they are, the easier your job will be.

Just like the Apostle, you will need to help Pastors not burn out in sheep-tending. You will likely see it coming before anyone, including the Apostle. Partner with the Apostle to keep the Pastors from burn out. Essentially, you are the pastor of the future of the community. You are the one who oversees the overseers, so your heart will blend with the Pastor's easily if you value and honor their ability to do what you do on a more personal, individual level. Train them in what you do and learn what they do. They know the sheep well and have a real grasp on how well you are doing. If they understand and trust you, they can help the sheep trust and follow your cultural sculpting.

The Prophet-Teacher relationship can be the most aggravating or the most fruitful relationship; it is your choice which one you want it to be. Your calling is to shift things; that does not happen if there is no quality system in place to support the shift. Just like you can see the big picture problems ahead, the Teacher can see the technical details that will affect and be affected by the shifting. Partner with them and have grace with them as you try to come up with real solutions, because they have unique challenges in conveying and implementing changes effectively. You need them to be on board with what you are saying, because they are in control of how well your future plans will work. Trust their competence and endorse their strategies.

When you have more than one Prophet in a community, things can get hairy. There is a reason that there was generally one main prophet that the King of Israel listened to – mixed signals are dangerous. Though both Prophets are hearing from God, their focus is on what God said to *them*. It is the responsibility of a messenger to faithfully carry their message regardless of other people's opinions. The mixed signals can come if multiple sources are blowing their trumpet as the most important trumpet. In the New Testament model of the prophetic ministry, Paul said that when one prophet is speaking and another gets a word, the first is to defer to the next (1 Corinthians 14:30). Honor those who come after you just like you would have liked those who came before you to honor you as you were growing into where you are now. Realize that you are not the only one who can see; you have blind spots. Don't be threatened by them. Work as a team to lead your community to its glorious destiny.

How an Evangelist Relates to the Other Four

If you are an Evangelist, you are a spokesman for your awesome community. Know your limitations and your strengths; do your part very well and get other people connected to the community, then get back out there and live the culture outside the walls of the community. You are a linker, a conduit to freedom. So your main objective is simply to be a great example of the community that you represent.

When you relate to the Apostle of your community, honor them for being such an important part of your calling. They created a place for you to get free and bring others to in order to get free. Make it your goal to be connected to and in agreement with the apostolic vision of the community. This will make you more effective in rightly portraying and living the culture outside the community. If you advertize something that isn't real, people will blame you for false advertizing. So know whom you are serving under. Trust them. Honor them. Understand them.

In the same way that you need to know, understand, and believe in the apostolic vision of the community, you need to be connected to and in agreement with the prophetic direction of the community. That is the Prophet's world, but it is a huge part of who you are, as well. A vision for a community can get old or seem boring at times, but the Prophet provides the inspiring direction and movement to the community. Get to know them and feed off of the excitement that is all around them as they help to provide movement and a hopeful future to the community. You will help them by providing new fish in the boat; they will help you by giving a good reason to get in the boat.

The Evangelist is generally the first touch point of the culture to new people. Thus the Evangelist is a kind of pre-Pastor. This means that if you are an Evangelist, you need training and discipleship from the Pastor so that you know how to do what the Pastor does and carry his same heart for the people. This will make you more effective as an Evangelist because you will also know how to best integrate and connect new people into the heart of the community. The Pastor is a master at managing the hearts of the community. They likely have something that will help you in connecting to the people who will best fit into the community. Additionally, the Pastor really is the carrier of the heart of the culture. Apostles and Prophets maintain and sculpt the culture, but you need to be linked with the one who produces and monitors the pulse of the community to stay alive yourself and give you heart-fuel to draw people into that community.

The Evangelist is also the first touch some people have to a real Teacher. You have to carry a little bit of what the Teacher has; this will keep you solid, grounded, and have structures to help facilitate the care of those you are drawing. As much as you may want to just inspire people and draw them in, if you do not appreciate and understand the work that the Teacher does, your fresh fish will jump out of the boat or rot if you do not steward them rightly. This means connecting with the Teacher to help them create programs and structures to help you integrate new people quickly and effectively into the community. It takes time for adopted children to pick up on the flow and functions of the family.

Just like each of the Five have unique functions, so individual Evangelists have specific tendencies towards drawing people from certain realms of society and innate giftings that enable them to effectively draw people. Learn to rejoice in other Evangelists' styles and purposes. Don't try to be them, do things their way, or make them conform to your ways. Serve them, be excited about their contribution, and find a way to compete with them in a way that spurs each other on while staying in unity and deep affection.

How a Pastor Relates to the Other Four

Pastors, you are the circulatory system of the Body. You connect people to the heart and life of the community. Just because you see a gap or problem that does not mean that you need to be the answer to that issue. What it does mean is that you are responsible to bring life to the areas in need of life. You know your community intimately and you are vital to healthy Body life. Do your job well and raise up Pastors around you so that you can be more effective with less work.

When relating to your Apostle, be sure to honor the vision that they carry. Be as helpful to them as you can in letting them know how well the community is receiving the vision. This means that you need to be fundamentally in agreement with the vision that the Apostle has so that you can help the people you are shepherding to connect at a heart level with the apostolic vision. You are like the heart. Your job is to bring oxygen-rich blood to the parts of the body. But you also pull the used and tired blood to the liver to be cleaned. The Apostle needs you as a partner, not a critic. Be careful not to get frustrated with how "unrealistic" or "disconnected" they *seem* to be. Your job is to bridge that gap.

Because Prophets generally see things out ahead of the community and make corporate direction changes, it is vital that you be in unity with the Prophet. This is a two way street. They need your input as overseer into what is currently going on in the corporate heart, but you need to trust that the Prophet can see things that you cannot. Your perspective is supposed to be on a more "down to earth" or ground level so that you can help the individuals and the heart of the community; Prophets are not meant to be kind pediatricians or family doctors, they are trained surgeons. When they see a needed shift, your job is to help the community make that shift in their hearts. This will require flexibility in your own heart because you will be the first to have to make the switch before you can help others make the transition. The more connected you are to the Prophet, the more you will each take on each others' natures and be a better team.

Evangelists will keep you from ever being bored. New sheep in the flock means a lot of work for the shepherd, but if you can train the Evangelists to pastor the sheep before they enter the fold, then you simplify your process. Know your Evangelist-partner; they need your attention, approval, and perspective. They do not want to take care of the fish, but they are great at catching them – let them do their job. You need to know from them how to best partner with them to adopt the new people into your family.

As we have discussed, and as you probably have observed, much of Western Christianity has blended the Pastor and Teacher. If you are truly of the Pastor Tribe as we have defined it, then you really need a good Teacher to partner with to more fully care for your sheep. Teachers are brilliant organizers. Use them to promote the values and heart of the community that it needs to survive. They are the nervous system that gets ideas and actions to respond correctly in the body. Value their contribution in the community, for they hold everything together, have probably thought through many future problems, and have contingency plans to keep things flowing smoothly.

Pastors get along really well together, until suspicion gets into the heart. Your job is to protect your flock, if someone else comes in with a heart for your same flock, don't get territorial. You have just doubled the number of eyes available and the perspectives on the flock. This is a good thing. This can make your job easier and you can carry each others' burdens when the sheep wear one of you out. Respect their ability and passion to care for the sheep. Feed off of each other. Thrive.

How a Teacher Relates to the Other Four

If the Pastor is the circulatory system, the Teacher is the nervous system of the Body. It is the Teacher who makes things work right, keeps things in order, and finds creative solutions when some circuit is not firing correctly. Like the brain, which finds alternate routes for synaptic connections when part of the brain is damaged, the Teacher is a problem-solver. If you find yourself most closely identifying with the Teacher, your function in your community is to assist others in fulfilling their functions most efficiently and at the highest level of dynamic excellence. This doesn't feel like pressure to you, it is what makes you come alive.

As you interact with Apostles, you will have to fight hard to stay teachable. Apostles are the ones responsible before God for the community they lead; your function as it relates to them is to honor the burden they carry, understand what the vision is, and do your best to transmit the vision from the head to the masses. Sometimes this will come through actual teaching, sometimes through creating systems or programs that support the apostolic vision. You are a transmitter of the Apostle's ideas – no matter how nebulous they seem. This will require patience to slow down and understand the Apostle so that you can take the ethereal and manifest it clearly and materially.

Likewise, with the Prophet, you will need to hear, listen, and understand the directions of the Prophet so that you can be the practical link between the prophetic leader and the way it touches the details of the community. Even more with the Prophet than the Apostle, you will need to be patient and understand. Initially their directions may seem unrealistic, unreasonable, or unnecessary. Regardless of your opinion on the matter, your job is to line up with the Prophet's direction and help everyone else do the same. This means that you will constantly be the first to have to make the internal mental shifts; go through this process *with* the Prophet. They have had to do the same thing already and will be key in helping you. Resist getting critical of them. If their culture-shifting directions fail, it is not because they aren't doing their job, it is because you have not done yours. Assist them in helping the community, and it will make your life smoother.

You are the Evangelist's net-maker to catch the fish and their fence-maker to house the new sheep. Partner with them to develop effective community programs and structural systems to help disciple and integrate the new people that come in from the work of the Evangelist. You create the landing pads for these fresh disciples to come in and be transformed in the way they live and how they understand their world. You help them renew their minds and adapt their behavior to reflect the culture of the Kingdom.

Though most Western churches combined the Pastor and Teacher, it is important to realize that they are very different and have different foci. Whereas you care about people thinking and living right, the Pastor cares deeply about hearts in the community. You will need to assist the Pastor in creating structures that will support a community with a healthy corporate heart. A Pastor can tend to be so focused on the individual people that the systems they would set up could actually hinder the kind of growth that they are intending to foster. You will know you are being effective in helping the Pastor when you work out the kinks in the community that have been compromising the spiritual integrity of the culture. This will be easily seen in the happiness and "family feel" of your community as it constantly grows.

In case you haven't yet caught onto this, you are mostly a helper. Jesus said that the Father was going to send the Helper, the Holy Spirit, who will lead you to all truth and will bring to remembrance everything that He had taught them (John 14:26 and John 16:13). This is one of the ways that you are like God; you are like the Holy Spirit in that you help others find Truth that sets them free (John 8:32). You help them understand and remember the things He has taught them. The accusation against Teachers is generally that they are "too heady," and that is not true. You are dynamic and selfless. Serve like God serves us.

When you encounter other Teachers, rejoice with each other and celebrate each other's brilliance. Fight for unity, because if you each have different ideas, competition will actually hinder your effectiveness. God's word through Isaiah is especially true of you; if one Teacher can transform a tiny community, two Teachers can transform an enormous community (Isaiah 30:17).

They Know We Are Christians by Our Honor

It is important to apply these principles to our own lives before we can start to hold others to a standard that we are not living up to (Matthew 7:3). But it is also important to recognize that Jesus instructed us to love our neighbors as ourselves (Mark 12:31). The prerequisite to loving others is to love ourselves. Towards the end of his life, Jesus' closest disciple (John), having walked with Him for decades after living with Him for 3 years, said that our ability to love comes from first receiving love from Love Himself (1 John 4:19). So if we are to fulfill His command to love others, we must first receive His love so that we know what real love is like.

To most fully appreciate, honor, and love others, our first task is to find out from our Creator what He appreciates, honors, and loves about us. This is a truly humbling encounter. Once we know what we were designed for, then we can start to understand how we fit in with the rest of the puzzle. Knowing our own identity frees us up to see others correctly and honor them with no need to compete or compare. This is an essential step in the process of taking over the world in preparation for the Coming of our King.

If the view the world has of us has anything but honor, love, unity, and hope attached to it, anything negative at all, we short-circuit our ability to free them. They will know we are Christians by our honor. The world thinks that they have love, but they have a weak echo of Love. What really messes with people that think Christians are judgmental, negative, hypocritical and myopic is when we judge them rightly, have a positive opinion of them, practice the Love we preach and have a grasp of the bigger picture. This happens when we honor each other and even honor those who are not "with us." True honor is fueled by love.

Nathan Scott, a friend and mentor of mine, always says that praise is shown in words but honor is displayed by actions. It is one thing for God to say that He loves the world, but it is an entirely more real statement when He sends His only Son to be slaughtered so that Jesus' murderers might become His Family. In our lives, it is no different. People will be drawn into our communities not because we constantly say nice things about them, but because they see that people in our communities are honored and celebrated for who they are. The world expects rejection from us. When we lovingly embrace everyone extravagantly, it speaks stronger than words.

One of the best techniques for corporate evangelism is happy and empowered people. Anyone who sees a group of people who enjoy each other and who gladly and frequently celebrate each other's strengths while covering their weaknesses will be drawn to such a loving family. This is not only our goal, but it is our calling. This is what the Kingdom looks like. Heaven does not look at you and see your sin, your habits, or your failures; Heaven sees the future you, the whole you, the real you.

Be wise. Agree with Heaven.

My Natural Tribe – part 2: Determining Which One Fits You

Remember, this isn't who you are, this is a way to understand who you are

You are not what you do. You are you.

Too often with personality tests, people get wrapped up in categorizing and lose sight of why profiling can be helpful. The purpose of this book and others like it is not to back you into a corner and force you to be a certain thing. That is not freedom, and the Gospel is about freedom. The purpose is to help you understand yourself and others a little bit more.

You are not one of the Five only. You may lean towards one or two of them primarily, but you are not stuck in that category for the rest of your life. You will find yourself acting like each one in different situations, depending on the circumstances and the people present. When I was the Student Pastor at MorningStar University, I found myself acting and thinking more like a Pastor. "Pastor" is not my Main Tribe. When I have been under strong apostolic authority where there is no Prophet functioning, I have found myself filling the role of Prophet. In writing this book, I have functioned as a Teacher. And at one point in my life I was a graphic designer and did a lot of marketing, functioning and thinking like an Evangelist to draw people to the culture that I was representing. But in all of these, I always leaned heavily toward an Apostolic mentality in those roles, because that is a core part of who I am – my Main Tribe.

As I have shared this way of thinking with others, it has helped us to understand ourselves, have grace for our short-comings, and embrace our need for the input of other people. That is the reason I wrote this book and have taught these principles, so that people can understand themselves a little more and thereby be more effective as people. There are dozens of other personality profile systems that are just as thorough and helpful. I encourage you to utilize those as you run across them.

Do not try to fit yourself into one of the Five. Discover which of the Five fits you best. When Paul wrote to the Ephesians, he said that the Five were given to people to serve and equip them. He did not say that people were to serve or exalt the Five. So it is with our current look at the Five as Tribes, they are there to serve you in discovering the glories hidden inside of you.

"Why?" and Other Questions That Will Help Bring Clarity

There are certain key questions you can ask that, when answered honestly, can illuminate how to apply this perspective on the Five. Here are a few of those questions, with some explanation on how the question can help you. These questions will help by getting you to boil down what is inside of you.

Question #1: "Why?"

This is the ultimate question. You could ask this simple question over and over to boil your motivation down and eventually find what drives you and see which of the Five matches up with you best. For example, if your 'ultimate *why*' has to do with people, then the Evangelist, Pastor, or Teacher will fit you better. But if you are mostly motivated by the blueprints of Heaven and "people just need to line up with Heaven," then the Apostle or Prophet probably fits you better. Keep in mind that neither of these is better, they all need each other. Being people-focused does not make someone anti-Heaven or un-spiritually-minded. The unfiltered answers to these questions will reveal what you value and thereby clarify your identity.

Question #2: "Who do you want to be?"

God has hidden your destiny inside of you, and He has concealed it in your internal mirror. There is something in you that only you can see, a potential inside that echoes through your whole being. No one can give it to you; He spoke it into you before you were born. Prophetic words can only confirm it to you. One day, in the age to come, Jesus will speak a name to you that only He knows you by and suddenly you will be fully known correctly. This person that you are becoming is how you see yourself. When someone treats you like anything else, it offends something in you, because you know deep inside that you are something different. This is why it is crucial to know and guard and understand our identities, so that we can celebrate who He has made us to be.

Question #3: "Who are your heroes?"

This is a lot like #2, or rather it can help you answer #2. The people who we look up to, our heroes and role models, earned that place in our hearts and opinions because there was something about them that reminds us of our internal mirror. Our heroes are foreshadows of who we are becoming. Think of Elijah and Elisha. Elisha wanted to be just like Elijah, and because he honored and served him to the end of Elijah's days on earth, Elisha got a double portion of his anointing (2 Kings 2). We value in others what we want to become. If something inspires you, that is an indication that you have an open door in the Lord to pursue that thing and assimilate that attribute of the Lord into who you are – or perhaps it is less of an assimilation and more of an activation. For years, I have told people I disciple, "Act today like the person you are becoming." Sure, we will make mistakes, but we can speed up our maturation process. God has given you everything you need for life and godliness (2 Peter 1:3). As we come to fully believe this, we will begin to live like we have what we need. This will change how we relate to God; we will not beg God to transform us but will rather lean into who He made us to be. Be your own hero. Act like the real you, not the old you.

Question #4: "What do you want to accomplish?"

Your passions can tell you a lot about your calling and your identity. God buried passions inside of you that He crafted for the world around you. These passions that He planted in you were designed specifically for you, because He created you uniquely to be the optimal carrier of those particular passions. They are ultimately *His* passions, and therefore are part of His personality that He put inside of you. If you recognize what you want to accomplish, it can be an indicator of your destiny. Within the community that you find yourself, what do you want to accomplish? Do you want to be sure that people around you feel safe and free? That is a Pastoral passion. Do you want to create incredibly effective and dynamic systems that will help people succeed? That is a Teacher's heart. Are you passionate about keeping people from fruitlessness and help get people on the right track by avoiding obvious potholes in the road ahead of them? That is what Prophets live for. You get the point.

Question #5: "When do you feel most alive?"

This gives another shade to #4, but takes it out of the realms of our lives that could be merely "vain ambitions." Do you feel alive when you are in the middle of a community, inspiring people to give their time and energy to what is being built? That is what makes Apostles come alive. Do you feel a pull to always tell people about great things that you have experienced so that they can experience it as well? That gives life to Evangelists. Do you feel invigorated when you are learning something and you are simultaneously looking for ways to pass on your understanding? Teacher. If everyone lived from a place of what brings life to him or her, the world would be a much different place. People would be happier, fulfill their purposes, and we would fit together rightly. We are safest when we are in the center of our purpose in God, who is the Tree of Life, the place where we can truly be Eternally alive.

What Doesn't Matter: Giftings, Functions, Positions, and Opinions

Inevitably, people will read this book and realize that they are out of alignment with what is inside of them. But life circumstances can easily deter us from making the changes necessary to be happy and effective. It will not always be an easy transition. There will be obstacles. But, just like the seven churches in Turkey that Jesus sent messages to in Revelation 2 and 3, there is a reward for those who overcome. But we must take courage and lay aside the things that entangle us and are irrelevant distractions in our lives.

Your natural giftings do not dictate which of the Five Tribes you associate with most strongly. You may be very proficient at teaching. People may automatically categorize you as a Teacher. That does not, however, mean that you are a Teacher. You may be reading this book and find that you feel drawn to and associate most with the Prophet described herein. Your gifting is secondary to your identity.

Your function or position in a community does not determine your Tribe. You may function in the role of a "head pastor" of a church, but deep inside of you there is this burning desire to just get out and bring people into the family. You are of the Evangelist Tribe. You just happen to have found yourself in an occupational position meant for an Apostle (even though we call it "head pastor"). Your position doesn't necessarily need to change, but the application of your identity and your perspective on yourself, others, and your own life may need to shift.

The most prevalent factor is also the least important: other people's opinions of who you are. It doesn't matter what people think you are, you must know who you are from the One who created you in the first place. People may have a very strong opinion of you, that you are an Apostle. They may even use *this book* to convince you. But you know that you are a Prophet. Guess who is right...you.

Ultimately, you will have to let go of every factor that influences your belief structures and embrace Truth. Whether it is in regards to our identity, our church structures, our theology, our purpose or our assignment in God, everything must submit to Truth. The Man who is Truth incarnated is the King before whom we bow.

My Resonant Frequency: We Are Who We Believe Jesus Told Us We Are

In my early twenties, I was a worship leader at a small ministry in Lansing, Michigan. Two of my best friends were worship leaders with me. One of those friends was incredibly obsessed with sound engineering and music production; the other is easily the most dynamic lyricist and songwriter that I know. It was quite an experience doing life with them.

My sound-obsessed friend was always tinkering with the sound system. He would spend his own money to get equipment that would improve the experience of the worshipers; and then he would spend hours tweaking that equipment to get everything just right. On one occasion, I came to the ministry early for practice only to find he was working on the new bass amps. He excitedly told me to stand in the middle of the room. He adjusted the soundboard and went to the stage. He plucked one note and the whole building seemed to shake. I asked what on earth he had done to make it feel like every particle in the room was vibrating at the same time. He said, "I found the resonant frequency of the room!"

He continued by explaining to me that the acoustics of every room were different and that it is possible to find the exact note that will resonate with the way the room is shaped and set up. He had found the precise frequency that matched the sanctuary. He did not even have to play the note loudly; it matched the inside of the building and that frequency made every air molecule and object seem to vibrate with life. It was like hearing the perfect harmony in a song, but it wasn't voices, it was the room itself. I have never experienced anything like that before or since. It was surreal.

In the same way, when Jesus speaks our identity into us, it resonates with us. Some people may take a guess, saying that we are a "D-Sharp", and they would be close to right. My friend found the frequency exactly, and it was not a perfect note. He had to tune his guitar string off of a "normal" tuning. Someone may have always told you that you are a pastor, but it never sat right with you. Maybe it wasn't completely off, but it just didn't quite ring true for you. Maybe you are actually a Teacher that is very pastoral or has a pastoral position. Or maybe people have labeled you an evangelist, you have that title in your community, and you have functioned like that for years. You may have even come to terms with that as true. But as you have been reading, your heart jumps out of you when reading about the Apostle.

The bottom line is that who Jesus says you are is the truth. He is your Maker and knows you better than you know yourself. And even if you do not like or value what He calls you, when He speaks it, it vibrates inside in a way that you cannot deny and cannot ignore. No one can convince you of anything else once you have heard the Creator's voice speak your true name. It is an addictive, haunting encounter that I pray you are soon afflicted with. An encounter like that will liberate you and resurrect you in areas of your life that you may have never recognized were in need of such an experience.

You Might Be A ___________ If...

If you have ever seen the old school comedians, you are familiar with the "You might be a redneck if..." jokes. Here are some statements in that vein regarding the Five Tribes.

You might be an Apostle if...

...you consistently find yourself in the center of a community, making decisions that affect everyone around you.

...you feel like you are being ineffective in a community if you cannot help make major changes to propel the community forward.

...your friends and family call you "stubborn" because you are unmoving on how things are supposed to be, yet you and they both know that your way really is the better way, though rarely the easiest.

You might be a Prophet if...

...you can see opportunities and ambushes months before those around you; and though people have called you a pessimist, you're just reporting what you think should be obvious to everyone else.

...you get accused of being critical, but it doesn't matter to you, because you know that your heart is to help people get to the right place and avoid the land mines.

...you think you are communicating something clearly, but people look at you funny because they cannot understand what seems plain and simple to you.

You might be an Evangelist if...

...you are easily excited about something, but rarely satisfied with settling down and staying put.

...your friends expect you to know what the group should go do for fun, because you always have a fresh new idea of fun activities.

...you are constantly and unintentionally giving companies free advertising by recommending their products and services after just one good experience.

You might be a Pastor if...

...you find yourself less concerned about the result or success of a project than how it will affect the people involved.

...you have been called a "people pleaser" or been accused of catering to the needs of people, and though those comments were intended to be a correction, you took them as a compliment secretly in your heart.

...you miss deadlines and schedules because you are spending time with people in need of relational ministry – staying last at parties and services.

You might be a Teacher if...

...you have a detailed solution to problems before someone even finishes explaining the situation (or maybe even before they talk to you).

...you love to study, teach, and train, but if someone asks you a personal question or opens up about their feelings you freak out a little inside and force an attentive look on your face (the whole time frantically searching for a problem to solve).

...you find it difficult to view the Song of Songs as a love story from Jesus to His Bride (the Church) because in your mind it is simply a poem describing King Solomon's love life.

In the Mirror: Rejoicing in Who You Are

Loving Yourself: The Assumption After the Greatest Commandment

When Jesus was asked which of the Scriptural Commandments was the Greatest, His answer was to love God fully (Matthew 22:36-38). But He followed this obvious answer with a curious addition. He said that the second greatest commandment was to "love your neighbor the same way that you love yourselves." This was not a curious statement at face value, but the assumption that He was making between the Greatest and Second Commandment was that we love ourselves. Though on the surface of our narcissistic society we seem to really love ourselves, the sad truth is that at the core of the self-indulgence is a profound self-hatred. We can soften its name and call it a "rejection spirit," but painting a coffin a pretty color does not alter its contents.

Self-view is under attack, particularly in the parts of society that have a conservative religious background. Let's assume for just a moment that we truly did love ourselves, and that our Western First World pampering is not self-indulgence but rather a manifestation of our agreement with God's opinion of us. Then the challenge from Jesus is to treat everyone you know the same way you treat yourself. But for the rest of us, who are masquerading our emotional masochism around as humility or disguising it with religious make-up, Jesus is challenging us to *actually* love ourselves.

Now it is fascinating, if you slow down and read this passage, Jesus says that the Second Commandment is *like* the First. In other words, there is a similarity between loving God and loving our neighbor. The connection is: loving the Image of God. And since you also carry the Image of God, the Assumption implies that you must love yourself like you love God. The Assumption and the Second Commandment are natural next steps after the Greatest Commandment. In the very acts of us loving God, He creates in us a love for ourselves and our neighbor simply by being touched by what Brennan Manning calls "the furious longing of God."

Love is not mere lip service. Love is actions, words, thoughts, and emotions towards someone. If that "someone" is you, then your actions towards yourself should reflect the love you have for God in you. The way you talk about yourself must line up with how you would talk about Jesus Himself. Likewise your thoughts, assumptions and feelings about yourself must have a divine, eternal perspective. We have to appreciate ourselves, value ourselves and even – dare I say it? – *like* ourselves.

By understanding yourself, specifically how God has formed you, you can step into the Second Commandment. This book can help to empower you to appreciate, value, and like those around you far more than you already do. The freedom this book has given you is transferable. There is an old saying: "hurt people will hurt people." Verily, verily I say unto thee: freed people free people.

Be free and be a freer.

Pressure-Free Identity: The Best You There Is

The brilliance of God is displayed in the uniqueness of each of His children. He can love everyone fully and differently, simply because no two of us are the same. No one is being compared to anyone else. There is no "better you" that He is holding your life up next to, seeing if you are improving, measuring up, or remaining stagnant. God doesn't even think like that. He puts no pressure on you to be a better you. He didn't ask you to clean up your life to come to Him, He just invited you to His table because He saw that you were hungry.

You are the best you there is.

Now, before you say "I'm the only me," realize that there is a dead you and a living you. The dead you cannot be sanctified, is not seated in the Heavenly place, and will never see God. But the real, living you can, is, and will.

Will you grow more mature, more like Jesus? Most likely, yes.

Will that make you more desirable to God? No. He loved you before you started trying to "fix" yourself, before you gave up and let Him transform you, and before you even knew He was doing anything in your life.

There is no future you. There is only the dead you that died on the Cross with Jesus and the living you that is reading these words right now. The living you is fully endorsed by God. You are awesome. You are powerful. You are just like Jesus in a way that no one else can be. You are the best you there is.

The only way to improve the living you is to be more fully you and less like anyone else. Be pure you, with no residue of anyone else or anything else.

I'm from Michigan. In Michigan, we know snow. When endeavoring to make a good snowball, you want to use the fluffy, fresh snow on top. This snow has never touched the ground, has nothing but snow in it. These are the BEST snowballs. They are pure snow, with no residue of the dirty ground, the twigs, or anything else. Just pure snow. Likewise, when we let go of our obsession with men of God and become obsessed with the God of men, we find that great men are still men. Our obsession then becomes a journey to be the greatest expression of Christ that we are able to manifest. We become that perfectly pure snow, having no residue from other people.

Even in that obsession, we can place pressure on ourselves to perform. But in Him, there is absolutely no pressure, only invitation. And here is the invitation: "Come." There is no front-loading or back-loading on the invitation. No "do this and then come." No "come, and then do this." It is simply "Come." He invites you to come and unashamedly be yourself. He loves how He made you, and He wants you with Him as He does what He does. He will open doors you would never have access to on your own. He will provide for each step you take with Him, not because He is obligated as "the God who provides" but because He is a good Father and a good Master.

You cannot be me any better than I can be you. We would each make a horrible substitute for the other. Maybe we should just agree to embrace our identities unreservedly. Maybe we should enjoy our own paths. Maybe that person in the mirror is greater than we have been led to believe.

Self-Expression Without Self-Evaluation: Fearlessly Living Out Matthew 18:3

Ultimately, the difficulty we have in fully living in our identity is more of an internal issue than the result of external limitations. Though we would sometimes like to be able to blame other people for our inability to be ourselves, whether people from our past or present, the stunning reality is that others can only hinder you if you allow them to. People have only as much authority in your life as you allow them to have, based on your relationship to them and to intermediaries. If someone is keeping you from walking in your fullness, it is because you are allowing them access to the control of your life in some way or another. The next step for you is to take control of yourself...have *self-control.*

Once other people are out of the way in your own mind, the real battle begins. We are usually our own worst critics. But there is hope. Have you ever noticed the exponential growth of self-criticism? Babies do not evaluate themselves. Children do not evaluate themselves. Teenagers start to evaluate themselves. Adults are the professional self-haters. Teens generally learn their self-evaluation skills from adults in their lives. We must return to being like children again!

Matthew's gospel quotes Jesus as saying, "unless you are converted and become like children, you will not enter the Kingdom of Heaven" (Matthew 18:3). The word that Matthew uses here means 'to turn around'. Think of it this way: if your life is a walk down a path and you find that you are far down the path, in order to enter the Kingdom, you will have to turn around and go back to the side trail that you saw towards the beginning of your journey. That is the Kingdom Trail, the child's path.

Our minds need to be made new again – to be re-*new*-ed. Our desperate need is to see ourselves as children, think like children, and make decisions like children. I lived with a family of five for a while. When their oldest son Judah was 2 years old, he started exploring acrobatics like little boys do. When he would jump off the back of the couch, he did not think about how it may affect his joints or if it would hurt when he hit the floor. His thoughts went something like this: "I have seen cartoons where people fly, I suppose I should be able to fly. This couch will have to do as my jump point, because it is the highest thing I can find to climb right now." When Judah started a fight with me, he was not weighing the risk-reward ratio or considering his size and my intelligence. His one thought was, "This is going to be fun."

It becomes clear that we have rejected our "adult maturity" when we have the freedom to live wildly in our self-expression. Abandoned to our enjoyment of life, we look more to the moment and less to the repercussions. We eventually forget to doubt ourselves, whether due to confidence in our Father's protection or because we finally believe that we are equipped and qualified in Him.

As renewed children, we begin to simply act and trust. If there is evaluation, it is retrospective and objective. Whereas in our pseudo-maturity we would faithlessly confabulate before acting, hesitate in self-doubt while acting, and exaggerate in our negative critiquing of our past actions. The purpose of evaluation is for improvement, but it has become a temple to the idol of self-hatred. Freedom from such self-deprecating internal masochism transforms into a wild and unbridled delight in full abandonment to the God of all Pleasure.

Selflessness: The Original Purpose of The Five

In the pursuit of rejoicing in who you are, it is important to not slip into an extreme and forget that the whole purpose of the Five was to serve and accelerate the rest of the Body. Paul says that God gave the Five "for the equipping of the saints." In other words, the reason God crafted people with unique giftings, talents and personalities is so that those around them can benefit from what He put inside of them. This is why it is so ludicrous for people to covet these positions in churches. It isn't until you get into an official position that you realize that being a pastor is not a place of power; it is a place of extreme weakness. Being a prophet is not a position of influence; it is a place of supreme responsibility. James says that teachers will be judged more strictly than others (James 3:1). Evangelists are some of the most rejected people in churches and in the world. And if you want to know what it takes to become an apostle, read Paul's credentials in Second Corinthians.

The purpose of the Five, really the purpose of Christianity, is intentional selflessness. The invitation that God extends to us has one message, but two ways of expressing it. On one side of the invitation it reads, "Come, live." On the other side of the invitation it reads, "Come, die." Really, depending on the season you are in, one side or the other will be a better expression of what the Lord is inviting us into. He came to give us life abundant. True. He has called us to die to ourselves over and over. Also true. Particularly in places of leadership, it is our increasing responsibility to die to our needs and prefer others far above ourselves.

Understanding your Main Tribe is simply a revelation of how you are predisposed to serving others. You are uniquely crafted to support others in a way that only you can. Having come to understand the Five, we cannot hold other people to the standard we now have set up for ourselves. Rather, we must apply our understanding in a way that empowers, rejoices in and accelerates others into their glorious identity. You now have new tools to serve others with. Build up the body, and do not stop until we are all in the unity of the faith, the unity of the knowledge of Jesus, until we are a mature Bride for Christ, and have become overflowingly full of Christ's nature.

Freedom: Alpha and Omega, and Beta through Psi

The two most famous letters of the Greek language are Alpha and Omega. They are the beginning and end of the Greek alphabet, like our A and Z in English. Jesus describes Himself as the Alpha and the Omega in John's über vision we call the Book of the Revelation. But what is between A and Z is what really makes up the English language. Without B through Y we have a binary language, which works for computers, but not for humans. Our B is the Greek Beta and Psi is the letter just before Omega. It takes all of these letters to communicate what we are trying to communicate. In the same way, it takes the whole process of our lives to fully experience what God is trying to communicate to and through us.

Too often we see salvation as two bookends: the prayer we prayed to receive Jesus as Savior and His Second Coming redemption of humanity. Jesus, the Alpha and Omega, was filled with something. What was His Beta through Psi? Well, His name means Savior, Deliverer, Freer. Inside a Freer is freedom. The overflow of our lives is what fills us. And the overflow of His life was our freedom.

From beginning to end, the Gospel is about freedom. It is for freedom that we were set free. He initiated our freedom. He will increase our freedom in the process. And He will complete our freedom. We are freed so that we can make others free.

Apostles are freedom creators...

Prophets are freedom enforcers...

Evangelists are freedom demonstrators...

Pastors are freedom protectors...

Teachers are freedom designers...

Saints are freedom revolutionaries.

About the Author

Vince Corcoran is the Founder of Encounter Culture Ministries – an organization with the charge to create a culture of spiritual encounters with Jesus, but also the mandate from Jesus to "Go, encounter the culture around you."

A graduate of the Special Forces Missions program at MorningStar University, Vince was ordained by Rick Joyner after serving as Student Pastor and Student Life Director. He has traveled throughout the U.S. and internationally as a speaker and discipleship trainer, and recently as a church organizational consultant for new and developing churches.

Vince's highest value is friendship with Jesus and his goal in all things is to partner in the fulfillment of Revelation 11:15 – the transformation and preparation of our world for the Eternal Emperor and His divine leadership.

To schedule Vince Corcoran to speak at your church or for church consultation, email:

encountercultureministries@gmail.com

29324553R00090

Made in the USA
Charleston, SC
09 May 2014